Dedication

Moaz Safi Yousef al-Kasasbeh
May 29, 1988 – January 3, 2015

Copyright © 2022
Yatir Nitzany
All rights reserved
ISBN-13: 978-1951244590
Printed in the United States of America

CONVERSATIONAL ARABIC QUICK AND EASY

(Lebanese Dialect)

Part - 3

YATIR NITZANY

Foreword

For many years I struggled to learn Spanish, and I still knew no more than about twenty words. Consequently, I was extremely frustrated. One day I stumbled upon this method as I was playing around with word combinations. Suddenly, I came to the realization that every language has a certain core group of words that are most commonly used and, simply by learning them, one could gain the ability to engage in quick and easy conversational Spanish.

I discovered which words those were, and I narrowed them down to three hundred and fifty that, once memorized, one could connect and create one's own sentences. The variations were and are *infinite*! By using this incredibly simple technique, I could converse at a proficient level and speak Spanish. Within a week, I astonished my Spanish-speaking friends with my newfound ability. The next semester I registered at my university for a Spanish language course, and I applied the same principles I had learned in that class (grammar, additional vocabulary, future and past tense, etc.) to those three hundred and fifty words I already had memorized, and immediately I felt as if I had grown wings and learned how to fly.

At the end of the semester, we took a class trip to San José, Costa Rica. I was like a fish in water, while the rest of my classmates were floundering and still struggling to converse. Throughout the following months, I again applied the same principle to other languages—French, Portuguese, Italian, and Arabic, all of which I now speak proficiently, thanks to this very simple technique.

This method is by far the fastest way to master quick and easy conversational language skills. There is no other technique that compares to my concept. It is effective, it worked for me, and it will work for you. Just be consistent with my program. By learning these mere 350 words, which I will teach you in this book, you too will also succeed the way I and many, many others have. This book is *not* a grammar book, nor a phrasebook, it's purely meant to assist in aiding you to communicate in a foreign language.

Contents

Introduction to the Program 6
Office 8
School 14
Profession 20
Business 24
Sports 30
Outdoor Activities 34
Electrical Devices 38
Tools 42
Auto 44
Nature 47
Animals 53
Religion, Holidays, and Traditions 61
Wedding and Relationship 65
Politics 68
Military 74

Introduction to the Program

You have now reached Part 3 of Conversational Arabic Quick and Easy: Lebanese Dialect. In Part 1 you learned the 350 words that could be used in an infinite number of combinations. In Part 2 you moved on to putting these words into sentences. You learned how to ask for help when your house was hit by a hurricane and how to find the emergency services. For example, if you need to go to a hospital, you have now been provided with sentences and the vocabulary for talking to doctors and nurses and dealing with surgery and health issues. When you get to the hospital, you can tell the health services, "The hurricane caused a lot of destruction and damage in its path," and "We used the hurricane shelter for refuge."

In this third book in the series, you will find the culmination of this foreign language course that is based on a system using key phrases used in day-to-day life. You can now move on to further topics such as things you would say in an office. This theme is ideal if you've just moved for a new job. You may be about to sit at your desk to do an important task assigned to you by your boss but you have forgotten the details you were given. Turn to your colleagues and say, "I have to write an important email but I forgot my password." Then, if the reply is "Our secretary isn't here today. Only the receptionist is here but she is in the bathroom," you'll know what is being said and you can wait for help. By the end of the first few weeks, you'll have at your disposal terminology that can help reflect your experiences. "I want to retire already," you may find yourself saying at coffee break on a Monday morning after having had to go to your bank manager and say, "I need a small loan in order to pay my mortgage this month."

I came up with the idea of this unique system of learning foreign languages as I was struggling with my own attempt to learn a language. When playing around with word combinations I discovered 350 words that when used together could make up an infinite number of sentences. From this beginning, I was able to start speaking in a new language. I then practiced and found that I could use the same technique with other languages, such as French, Portuguese, Italian and Arabic. It was a revelation.

This method is by far the easiest and quickest way to master other languages and begin practicing conversational language skills.

The range of topics and the core vocabulary are the main components of this flawless learning method. In Part 3 you have a chance to learn how to relate to people in many more ways. Sports, for example, are very important for keeping healthy and in good spirits. The social component of these types of activities should not be underestimated at all. You will, therefore, have much help when you meet some new people, perhaps in a bar, and want to say to them, "I like to watch basketball games," and "Today are the finals of the Olympic Games. Let's see who wins the World Cup."

For sports, the office, and for school, some parts of conversation are essential. What happens when you need to get to work but don't have any clean clothes to wear because of malfunctions with the machinery. What you need is to be able to pick up the phone and ask a professional or a friend, "My washing machine and dryer are broken so maybe I can wash my laundry at the public laundromat." When you finally head out after work for some drinks and meet a nice new man, you can say, "You can leave me a voicemail or send me a text message."

Hopefully, these examples help show you how reading all three parts of this series in combination will prepare you for all you need in order to boost your conversational learning skills and engage with others in your newly learned language. The first two books have been an important start. This third book adds additional vocabulary and will provide the comprehensive knowledge required.

DISCLAIMER - The use of numerical symbols to identify Arabic accents, in English transliteration, is known as the Franco-Arabic technique. In which three "3" is used to signify aayin عين. Seven "7" is used to signify ha ح. Two "2" is to signify قاف a soft "اه". Five "5" to signify kha خ.

مكتب - Office

Boss - (male) Moudir مدير
Boss - (female) Moudira مديرة
Employee - Mwazzaf موظف
Employee - (fem) Mwazzafeh موظفة
Staff – Mwazzafin موظفين
Meeting – 2ijtime3 اجتماع
Conference room – 2oudit El 2ijtime3at أوضة الإجتماعات
Secretary - Secrétaire سكروتيري
Receptionist – 2este3lemet استعلامات
Schedule – Jadwal جدول
Calendar – Reznema رزنامة

My boss asked me to hand in the paperwork.
Moudiri talab menni sallim (to hand in) el wra2.
.مديري طلب مني سلّم الورق

Our secretary isn't here today. The receptionist is here but she is in the bathroom.
El secretaira manna hon lyom. El 2este3lemet hon bass layka bel 7emmem.
.السكرتيرة مانا هون اليوم، الاستعلامات هون بس ليكا بالحمام

The employee meeting can take place in the conference room.
2ijtime3 el mwazzafin rah ysir bi 2oudit el 2ejtime3at.
.اجتماع الموظفين رح يصير بأوضة الاجتماعات

My business cards are inside my briefcase.
Bita2et el 3amal bi chantiti.
.بطاقة العمل بشنطتي

The office staff must check their work schedule daily.
Mwazzafin el maktab lezim ychaykou 3ala jadwal el cheghel (work) kel yom.
.موظفين المكتب لازم يشيكوا على جدول الشغل كل يوم

Office

Supplies – Lawezim لوازم
Pen – 2alam قلم
Ink – 7eber حبر
Pencil – 2alam Rsas قلم رصاص
Eraser – Me77ayeh محاية
Desk - Maktab مكتب
Cubicle - Zewyeh زاوية
Chair – Kersi كرسي
Office furniture – Mafrouchet Maketib مفروشة مكتب
Business card – Bita2it 3amal بطاقة عمل
Lunch break – Forsit Ghada فرصة غدا
Days off – Forsa فرصة
Briefcase – Chanta شنطة
Bathroom – 7emmem حمام

I am going to buy office furniture.
Ana rayi7 2echtry mafrouchet maktab.
أنا رايح أشتري مفرشة مكتب.

There isn't any ink in this pen.
Ma fi 7eber bhal 2alam.
ما في حبر بهالقلم.

This pencil is missing an eraser.
2alam el rsas hayda na2sa (missing) menno el me77ayeh.
قلم الرصاص هيدا ناقصة منه المحاي.

Our days off are written on the calendar.
2eyem el foras taba3na maktoubin 3al reznema.
أيام الفرص تبعنا مكتوبين عالرزنامة.

I need to buy extra office supplies.
Lezim 2echtri zyedeh (extra/more) lawezim lal maktab.
لازم أشتري زيادة لوازم للمكتب.

I am busy until lunch.
Ana machghoul (busy) la wa2et el ghada.
أنا مشغول لوقت الغدا.

Laptop – Laptop لابتوب
Computer – Computer كمبيوتر
Keyboard – Keyboard كيبورد
Mouse – Mouse ماوس
Email – Email إيميل
Password – Kilmit morour كلمة مرور
Attachment – Murfa2 مرفق
Printer – Tabi3a طابعة
Colored printer – Tabi3a Mlawwaneh طابعة ملونة
Internet – Internet انترنت
Account – 7seb حساب
A copy - Naskha نسخة
To copy – Tensakh تنسخ
Paste – Telsi2 تلصق
Cut and paste – 2as w lasi2 قص ولصق
Fax – Fax فاكس
Scanner - Scanner سكانر
To scan – Ta3mol Scan تعمل سكان
Telephone – Telephone تليفون
A charger – Cha7en شاحن
To charge – Tich7an تشحن
To download – Ta7meel تحميل
To upload – Rafe3 رفع

I have to write an important email but I forgot my password for my account.
Lezim 2ektob email mhemm (important) bass nsit (forgot) kilmit el morour taba3 7sebi.
لازم أكتب إيميل مهم بس نسيت كلمة المرور تبع حسابي.

I need to purchase a computer, a keyboard, a printer, and a desk.
Lezim 2echtri computer, keyboard, tabi3a w maktab.
لازم أشتري كمبيوتر، كيبورد، طابعة ومكتب.

Where is the mouse for my laptop?
Wen el mouse taba3 el laptop taba3i?
وين الماوس تبع اللابتوب تبعي؟

Office

To download – Ta7meel تحميل
To upload – Rafe3 رفع
Internet – Internet انترنت
Account – 7seb حساب
A copy - Naskha نسخة
To copy – Tensakh تنسخ
Paste – Telsi2 تلصق
Cut and paste – 2as w lasi2 قص ولصق
Fax – Fax فاكس
Scanner - Scanner سكانر
To scan – Ta3mol Scan تعمل سكان
Telephone – Telephone تليفون
A charger – Cha7en شاحن
To charge – Tich7an تشحن

Where is my phone charger?
Wen el cha7en taba3 telephoni?
وين الشاحن تبع تليفوني؟
The scanner is broken.
El scanner manzou3a (broken).
السكنر منزوعة.
The telephone is behind the chair.
El telephone wara el kersi.
التليفون ورا الكرسي.
Do you have a colored printer?
3andak tabi3a mlawwaneh?
عندك طابعة ملونة؟
I needed to fax the contract but instead, I decided to send it as an attachment in the email.
Ken lezim 2eb3at el 3a2ed bel fax bass badal hek, 2arraret 2eb3ato murfa2 bel email.
كان لازم أبعت العقد بالفاكس بس بدل هيك قررت أبعته مرفق بالإيميل.
The internet is slow today therefore it's difficult to upload or download.
El internet bati2 (slow) lyom men hek so3b ta3mol ta7meel 2aw rafe3.
الانترنت بطيء اليوم من هيك صعب تعمل تحميل أو رفع.

11

Shredder – Ferrameh فرامة
Copy machine – Makanit Toswir ماكنة تصوير
Filing cabinet – Khzenit El Faylet خزانة الفايلات
Paper – Wara2 ورقة
Page – Saf7a صفحة
Paperwork – Tokhlis Wra2 تخليص ورق
Portfolio – Malaff ملف
Files – Malaffet ملفات
Document – Moustanad مستندات
Contract – 3a2ed عقد
Records – Sejellet سجلات
Archives – Archive أرشيف
Data – Bayenet بيانات
Analysis – Te7lil تحليل

The supervisor at our company is responsible for data analysis.
El mushref 3anna bel cherkeh (company) mas2oul 3an te7lil (analysis) el bayenet.
المشرف عنا بالشركه مسئوول عن تحليل البيانات.

The copy machine is next to the telephone.
Makanit el toswir 7add el telephone.
ماكنة التصوير حد التليفون.

The ruler is next to the shredder.
El mastara 7add el forrameh.
المسطرة حد الفرامة.

I can't find my stapler, paper clips, nor my highlighter in my cubicle.
Ma 3am le2i el kebbayseh, wala el attachet, wala el fluo bel zewyeh 3andi.
ما عم لاقي الكباسة ولا الأتاشيت ولا الفلو بالزاوية عندي.

The garbage can is full of papers.
Sallit el zbeleh maleneh wara2.
سلة الزبالة ملانة ورق.

Office

Deadline – Maw3ad Nihe2i موعد نهائي
Binder – Classeur كاسير
Paper clip – Attache أتاشي
Stapler - Kebbayseh كباسة
Staples – Khartouch Kebbayseh خرطوش كباسة
Stamp – Khatem ختم
Mail – Barid بريد
Letter - Riseleh رسالة
Envelope – Zaref ظرف
Highlighter - Fluo فلو
Marker - Fluo فلو
To highlight – Lawwin لَوِّين
Ruler – Mastara مسطرة

Give me the file because today is the deadline.
3tini (give me) el malaff la2enno lyom el maw3ad el nihe2i.
اعطيني الملف لأنه اليوم الموعد النهائي.

Where do I put the binder?
Wen b7ott el classeur?
وين بحط الكاسور؟

I need a stamp and an envelope.
Badi khatem w zaref.
بدي ختم و ظرف.

There is a letter in the mail.
Fi riseleh bel barid.
في رساله بالبريد.

The filing cabinet is full of documents.
Khzenit el filet maleneh (full) moustanadet.
خزانة الفايلات ملانة مستندات.

School - مدرسة

Student - Telmiz تلميذ
Student - (f) Telmizeh تلميذه
Teacher – 2estez أستاذ
Teacher – (f) M3allmeh معلمة
Substitute teacher – 2estez Badil أستاذ بديل
A class – Saff صف
A classroom – Saff صف
Education – Te3lim تعليم
Grade (level) - Saff صف
Grade (grade on a test) – 3alemeh علامة
Report card – Carnet كارنيت

The classroom is empty.
El saff fadi (empty).
الصف فاضي.

I want to bring my laptop to class today.
Badi jib el laptop 3al saff lyom.
بدي جيب اللابتوب عالصف اليوم.

Our math teacher is absent and therefore a substitute teacher replaced him.
2estez el math gheyib menhek 2eja ma7allo 2estez badil.
أستاذ الماث غايب من هيك أجا محله أستاذ بديل.

All the students are present.
Kel el tlemiz 7adrin.
كل التلاميذ حاضرين.

Make sure to pass your classes because you can't fail this semester.
T2akkad (make sure) enno tenja7 bi droosak la2enno mafik tos2ot hayda el fasel (semester).
اتأكد إنه تنجح بدروسك لأنه ما فيك تسقط هيدا الفصل.

You must get good grades on your report card.
Lezim tjib 3alemet meni7a (good) 3al carneh.
لازم تجيب علامات منيحة عالكرنيه.

School

Private school – Madraseh Khassa مدرسه خاصة
Public school – Madraseh Rasmiyeh مدرسه رسمية
Elementary school – Madraseh 2ebtide2yeh مدرسه ابتدائية
Middle school – Madraseh Metwasta مدرسه متوسطة
High school – Madraseh Sanawyeh مدرسة ثانوية
University – Jem3a جامعة
College – Kellyeh كلية
Grade (level) - Saff صف
Grade (grade on a test) – 3alemeh علامة
Report card – Carnet كارنيت
Pass – Neji7 نجاح
Fail – Sa2it سقوط
Absent - Gheyib غايب
Present – 7adir حاضر

The education level at a private school is much more intense.
Moustawa (level) el te3lim bi madraseh khassa mkassaf (intense) aktar bi ktir.
مستوى التعلم بمدرسة خاصة مكثف أكتر بكتير.

I went to a public elementary and middle school.
Re7et 3a madraseh 2ebtide2iyeh w madraseh metwasta.
رحت عمدرسة ابتدائية ومدرسة متوسطة.

I have good memories of high school.
3andi zekrayet 7elweh men el sanawyeh.
عندي زكريات حلوة من الثانوية.

My son is 15 years old and he is in the ninth grade.
2ebni 3omro 15 seneh w houeh bel saff el tesi3.
ابني عمره 15 سنة و هو بالصف التاسع.

College textbooks are expensive.
El ketob bel kellyeh ghalyin.
الكتب بالكليه غاليين.

I want to study at an out-of-state university.
Badi edros (to study) bi jem3a barrat (outside) el wileyeh (state).
بدي أدرس بجامعة برات الولاية.

Subject – Mawdou3 موضوع
Science – 3ouloum علوم
Chemistry - Chimia كيميا
Physics – Physia فيزيا
Geography – Joghrafia جغرافيا
History – Terikh تاريخ
Math – Math ماث
Addition – Jame3 جمع
Subtraction – Tare7 طرح
Division – 2osmeh قسمة
Multiplication – Dareb ضرب
Papers – Wra2 ورق
Folders – Malaffat ملفات

At school, geography is my favorite subject, English is easy, math is hard, and history is boring.
El joghrafia hyeh medti el moufaddaleh bel madraseh, el 2englizi hayyin, el math so3ib, wel terikh bi zahhi2 (boring).
الجغرافيا هيي مادتي المفضلة بالمدرسة، الإنجليزي هيّن، الماث صعب، والتاريخ بزهق.

After English class, there is physical education.
Men ba3d saff el 2englizi, fi (there is) sport.
من بعد الصف الإنجليزي في سبورت.

Today's math lesson is on addition and subtraction. Next month it will be division and multiplication.
Saff el math taba3 lyom houeih jame3 w tare7. El chaher el jeye bi sir 2osmeh w dareb.
صف الماث تبع اليوم هو جمع وطرح ، الشهر الجاي بصير قسمة وضرب.

The teacher wants to teach roman numerals.
El 2estez baddo y3allim el a7rof el roumeniyeh.
الأستاذ بده يعلم الأحرف الرومانية.

All my papers are in my folder.
Kel wra2i bel malaff.
كل ورقي بالملف.

School

Language - Legha لغة
English – Englizi إنجليزي
Foreign language – Legha Ajnabiyeh لغة أجنبية
Physical education – Sport سبورت
Chalk – Tabshour طبشور
Board – Lo7 لوح
Alphabet – 2abjadiyeh أبجدية
Letters – 2a7rof أحرف
Words – Kalimet كلمات
To review – Traji3 تراجع
Dictionary – 2amous قاموس
Detention – 7ajez حجز
The principle – El Moudir المدير
Notebook - Daftar دفتر
Calculator – Calculatrice كلكوليتريس

This year for foreign language credits, I want to choose Spanish and French.
Hayde el seneh lal crediyet taba3 el leghet el 2ajnabiyeh, baddi na22i 2espani w frensewi.
هيدي السنة للكردت تبع اللغات الأجنبية بدي أنقي إسباني وفرنساوي.

I want to buy a dictionary, thesaurus, and a journal for school.
Baddi 2echtri 2amous, 2amous moufradet, w majalleh lal madraseh.
بدي أشتري قاموس، قاموس مفردات، ومجلة للمدرسة.

The teacher needs to write the homework on the board with chalk.
El 2estez baddo yektob el fared 3al lo7 bel tabchoura.
الأستاذ بده يكتب الفرض عالوح بالطبشورة.

Today the students have to review the letters of the alphabet
Lyom el tlemiz baddon yraj3ou el a7rof el 2abjadiyeh.
اليوم التلاميذ بدن يراجعوا أحرف الأبجدية.

If you can't behave then you must go to the principal's office, and maybe stay after school for detention.
2eza ma fik tetsarraf (behave) meni7 (good) lezim trou7 3a maktab el moudir, w yemkin tdallak ba3d el madraseh ma7ajoz.
إزا ما فيك تتصرف منيح لازم تروح عمكتب المدير، ويمكن تضلك بعد المدرسة محجوز.

Test – Fa7es فحص
Quiz – 2ikhtibar اختبار
Lesson - Dares درس
Notes – Moula7azat ملاحظات
Homework - Fared فرض
Assignment - Mouhemmeh مهمة
Project – Mashrou3 مشروع
Pencil – 2alam Rsas قلم رصاص
Eraser – Me77ayeh محاية
Pen – 2alam قلم
Ink – 7eber حبر
Backpack – Chantit Daher شنطة ضهر
Book - Kteb كتاب
Lunchbox – Chantit 2akel شنطة أكل
Lunch – Ghada غدا
Crayons – 2lem Telwin قلم تلوين

Today, we don't have a test but we have a surprise quiz.
Lyom, ma-3enna (we don't have) fa7es bass 3enna 2ikhtibar faj2a (suprise).
اليوم ما عنا فحص بس عنا اختبار فجأة.

Are a pen, a pencil, and an eraser included with the school supplies?
El 2alam w 2alam el rsas w wel me77ayeh men domon (including) lawezim el madraseh?
القلم و قلم الرصاص والمحاية من ضمن لوازم المدرسة؟

You have to concentrate in order to take notes.
Lezim trakkiz la te2dir tekhod moula7azat.
لازم تركز لتقدر تاخد ملاحظات.

I forgot my lunchbox and crayons at home.
Nsit chantit el 2akel wel 2lem el talween bel bet.
نسيت شنطة الأكل وأقلام التلوين بالبيت.

For lunch, your children can purchase food at the cafeteria or they can bring food from home.
Lal ghada, el wled fiyon yechtrou akel men el cafeteria aw yjibou akel men el bet.
للغدا الأولاد فيون يختاروا أكل من الكفيتيريا أو يجيبوا أكل من البيت.

School

Glue – Telzi2 تلزيق
Adhesive tape – Telzi2 تلزيق
Scissors – M2ass مقص
Cafeteria – Cafeteria كفيتيريا
Kindergarten – Grand-Jardin جراند جاردن
Pre-school – Petit-Jardin بتت جاردن
Day care – Garderie جاردنري
Triangle - Mtallat مثلث
Square – Mrabba3 مربع
Circle – Douwayra دويرة
Notebook - Daftar دفتر
Calculator – Calculatrice كلكوليتريس

I need glue and scissors for my project.
Baddi telzi2 w m2ass lal machrou3 taba3i.
بدي تلزيق ومقص للمشروع تبعي.

I need tape and a stapler to fix my book.
Baddi telzi2 w kebbayseh la salli7 ktebi.
بدي تلزيق وكباسة لصلّح كتابي.

The school librarian wants to invite the art and music teacher to the library next week.
Mwazzaf el maktabeh baddo ye3zom 2estez el fann wel mousi2a 3al maktabeh jem3it el jeyeh.
موظف المكتبه بده يعزم أستاذ الفن والموسيقى عالمكتبه جمعة الجاي.

To draw shapes such as a triangle, square, circle, and rectangle is easy.
Ta tersom 2achkel (shapes) metel el mtallat, el mrabba3, el douwayra wel mistateel ktir hayyin.
تا ترسم أشكال مثل المثلث، المربع، الدويرة والمستطيل كتير هيّن.

During the week, my youngest child is at daycare, my middle one is in pre-school, and the oldest is in kindergarten.
Bi noss el jem3a, ebni el zghir bel garderie, el westani bel petit-jardin, wel kbir bel grand-jardin.
بنص الجمعه، ابني الزغير بالجاردري، والوسطاني بالبتت جاردن، والكبير بالجراند جاردن.

My notepad and calculator are in my backpack.
El pad wel calculatrice bi chantti.
الباد والكالكوليترس بالشنطة.

Profession - Mehneh مهنة

Doctor – 7akim حكيم
Nurse - Moumarrid ممرض
Nurse - (f) Moumarrida ممرضة
Psychologist – 2akhissa2i Nefseni أخصائي نفسي
Psychiatrist - 7akim Nefseni حكيم نفساني
Veterinarian – Baytari بيطري
Lawyer – Mou7ami محامي
Judge – 2adi قاضي
Pilot - Tiyarji طيرجي

What's your profession?
Shou mehentak?
شو مهنتك؟

I am going to medical school to study medicine because I want to be a doctor.
Ana rayih 3a madrasit el tobb la 2edros tobb la2enno 7ebib sir (to become) 7akim.
أنا رايح عمدرسة الطب لأدرس طب لأنه حابب صير حكيم.

There is a difference between a psychologist and a psychiatrist.
Fi fare2 (difference) ben el 2akhissa2i el nefseni wel 7akim el nefseni.
في فرق بين الأخصائي النفساني والحكيم النفساني.

Most children want to be an astronaut, a veterinarian, or an athlete.
2aktariyet el wled badon ysirou rouwwed fada, 7ekama baytariyeh, 2aw riyadiyyin.
أكترية الولاد بدن يصيروا رواد فضاء، حكما بيطريه أو رياضيين.

The judge spoke to the lawyer at the court house.
El 2adi 7eka ma3 el mou7ami bel ma7kameh (court house).
القاضي حكى مع المحامي بالمحكمة.

The police investigator needs to investigate this case.
Moufattich el chorta bado y7a22i2 (to investigate) bi hayde el 2adiyeh (case).
مفتش الشرطة بدو يحقق بهيدي القضية.

Being a detective could be a fun job.
Cheghel el mou7a22i2 yemkin ykoun cheghel bi salli.
شغل المحقق يمكن يكون شغل بسلّي.

Profession

Flight attendant – Moudifet Tayaran مضيفة طياران
Reporter - Mourasil مراسل
Journalist – Sa7afi صحفي
Electrician - Kahrabji كهربجي
Mechanic – Mécanicien ميكانيكن
Investigator – Moufattich مفتش
Detective – Mou7a22i2 محقق
Translator - Terjmen ترجمان
Translator - (f) Terjmen ترجمان
Producer - Mountij منتاج
Director – Moukhrij مخرج

The flight attendant and the pilot are on the plane.
Moudifet el tayaran wel tiyarji henneh 3al tiyyara.
.مضيفة الطيران والطيرجي هني عالطيارة
I am a certified electrician.
Ana kahrabji mou3tamad (certified).
.أنا كهربجي معتمد
The mechanic overcharged me.
El mecanicien daffa3ni-zyedeh (overcharged me).
.الميكنيكين دفعّني زياده
I want to be a journalist.
Badi koun sa7afi.
.بدي كون صحفي
The best translators work at my company.
2a7san (best) terejmeniyeh byechteghlou bel cherkeh ma3i.
.أحسن ترجمنية بيشتغلوا بالشركة معي
Are you a photographer?
2enta msawwir?
انتَ مصور؟
The author wants to write a book.
El mou2allif baddo yektob kteb.
.المؤلف بده يكتب كتاب
I want to find the directors of the company.
Badi le2i moudara el cherkeh.
.بدي لاقي مدير الشركة

Artist (performer) – Fannen فنان
Artist (draws paints picture) – Ressem رسام
Author – Mou2allif مؤلف
Author – (f) Mou2allifeh مؤلفة
Painter – Ressem رسام
Dancer – Ra2is رقاص
Dancer – (f) Ra2isa رقاصة
Writer - Ketib كاتب
Writer - (f) Ketibeh كاتبة
Photographer – Mousawwer مصور
A cook – Tebbakh طباخ
Waiter – Waiter ويتر
Bartender – Bartender بار تندر

The artist drew a sketch.
El ressem rasam rasmeh.
.الرسام رسم رسمة

The artist produced new artwork for her catalog.
El fanneneh 2antajit (produced) 3amal jdid lal catalog taba3a.
.الفنينيه أنتجت عمل جديد للكتالوج تبعا

I want to apply as a cook at the restaurant instead of as a waiter.
Badi 2addim 3ala wazifit (position) tebbakh bel mat3am badel waiter.
.بدي أقدم على وظيفة طباخ مطعم بدل الويتر

The gardener can only come on weekdays.
El bestanji fyo yeji bass bi 2iyem-el-jem3a (weekdays).
.البستنجي فيو يجي بس أيام الجمعة

Being a bartender isn't an easy job.
Cheghel el bartender manno cheghel hayyin (easy).
.شغل البار تندر منو شغل هيّن

I am a part-time painter.
Ana ressem bi dawem-jez2i (part time).
.أنا رسام بدوام جزئي

Profession

Barber – 7elle2 حلاق
Barber – (f) 7elle2a حلّاقة
Barber shop – Ma7al 7le2a محل حلاقة
Stylist – 7elle2 حلاق
Housekeeper – San3a صانعة
Maid – San3a صانعة
Caretaker – Concierge كنكريج
Farmer – Mouzeri3 مزارع
Gardner – Jnayneti جنيناتي
Gardner – Bestanji- بستنجي
Mailman – Se3i Barid ساعي بريد
A guard – 7aras حارس
A cashier – Cashier كاشير

I have to go to the barbershop now.
Lezim rou7 3an el 7elle2 halla2.
.لازم روح عالحلاق هلأ

Why do we need another maid?
Lech badna san3a tenyeh (another)?
ليش بدنا صانعة تانية؟

I need to file a complaint against the mailman.
Lezim 2addim chakwa (complaint) dodd se3i el barid.
.لازم قدم شكوى ضد ساعي البريد

She was a dancer at the theater play.
Kenit ra2isa bel masra7iyyeh.
.كانت رقاصة بالمسرحية

You need to contact the insurance company if you want to find another caretaker.
Lezim tottosil (to contact/reach) bi cherkit el 2assurance eza baddak tle2i gheir wali 2amr.
.لازم تتصل بشركة الأشورنس إذا بدك تلاقي غير ولي أمر

The farmer can sell us ripened tomatoes today.
El mouzeri3 fiyo ybi3na banadoura mestwiyeh (ripened) lyom.
.المزارع فيو يبيعنا بندورة مستوية اليوم

Business - Tijara تجارة

A business / company – Cherkeh شركة
Factory – Ma3mal معمل
A professional – Me7terif محترف
Position - Markaz مركز
Position - Wazifi وظيفة
Work, job – Cheghel شغل
Employee - Mwazzaf موظف
Employee - (f) Mwazzafeh موظفة
Manager – Moudir مدير
Manager – (f) Moudira مديرة
Management – 2idara إدارة
Owner – Sa7ib صاحب
Secretary – Secretaira سكرتيرة

I need a job.
Lezemni cheghel.
لازمني شغل.

She is the secretary of the company.
Hiyeh el secretaira taba3-el (of the/belonging to) cherkeh.
هي السكرتيرة تبع الشركه.

The manager needs to hire another employee.
El moudir baddo ywazzif mwazzaf teni.
المدير بده يوظف موظف تاني.

How much is the salary and does it include benefits?
2addeh el ma3ach w byotdamman ta2dimet?
أديه المعاش وبيتضمن تقديمات؟

Management has your resumé and they need to show it to the owner of the company.
El 2idara 3andon el CV taba3ak w baddon yfarjouwa (to show) la sa7ib el cherkeh.
الإدارة عندن السي في تبعك ، وبدن يفرجوا لصاحب الشغل.

I am at work at the factory now.
2ana bel cheghel bel ma3mal halla2.
انا بالشغل بالمعمل هلأ.

An interview – Mou2ebaleh مقابلة
Résumé – CV سي في
Presentation – 3ared عرض
Specialist – 2ikhtisasi اختصاصي
To hire - Twazzif توظف
To fire – Tech7at تشحط
Pay check – Check El 2abed شيك القبض
Income - Madkhoul مدخول
Salary – Ma3ach معاش
Insurance - Assurance أشورنس
Benefits – Ta2dimet تقديمات
Trimester - Fasel فصل
Budget – Mizeniyeh ميزانية
Net - Safi صافي
Gross – 2ejmeli إجمالي
To retire – Tet2e3ad تتقاعد
Pension – Ta2e3od تقاعد

In business, you should be professional.
Bel tijara, lezim tkoun me7terif.
بالتجارة لازم تكون محترف.

I am lucky because I have an interview for a cashier position today.
7azzi 7elou la2eno 3andi mou2ebaleh la wazifit cashier lyom.
حظي حلو لأنه عندي مقابلة لوظيفة كاشير اليوم.

Is the presentation ready?
El 3ared jehiz?
العرض جاهز؟

The first trimester is part of the annual budget.
2awwal fasel houeh jeze2 (part) men el mizeniyeh el sanawyeh (annual).
أول فصل هو جزء من الميزانية السنوية.

I have to see the net and gross profits of the business.
Lezim shouf el rebe7 (profits) el safi wel 2ejmeli taba3 el tijara.
لازم شوف الربح الصافي والإجمالي تبع التجارة.

I want to retire already.
Sar baddi 2et2e3ad ba2a.
صار بدي اتقاعد بقى.

Client - Zboun زبون
Client - (f) Zbouneh زبونة
Broker - Semsar سمسار
Salesperson – Biyye3 بياع
Salesperson – (f) Biyye3a بياعة
Realtor - Semsar سمسار
Real Estate – 3i2aret عقارات
A purchase - Chreyeh شراية
A lease – 2ajar أجار
To lease – Y2ajjir يأجر
To invest - Testasmir تستسمر
Investment – 2istismar استسمار
Economy – 2iktisad اقتصاد

The demand in the real estate market depends on the economy.
El talab bi sou2 el 3i2aret bye3temid (depending) 3al 2iktisad.
الطلب بسوق العقارات بعتمد عالإقتصاد.

If you want to sell your home, I can recommend a very good realtor.
2eza baddak tbi3 baytak, be2dir 2onsa7ak bi semsar ktir mni7.
إزا بدك تبع بيتك بقدر أنصحك بسمسار كتير منيح.

The investor wants to invest in this shopping center because he says it has good potential.
El mestasmir bado yestasmir bi markaz el tasawwo2 hayda la2enno 3am 2oul 3ando 2edra.
المستثمر بدو يستثمر بمركز التسوق هيدا لأنه عم يقول عنده قدرة.

The value of the property increased by twenty percent.
2imet el 3i2ar (property) zedit (increased) 3echrin bel-miyyeh (percent).
قيمة العقار زادت عشرين بالمية.

How much is the commission on the sale?
2addeh el commission 3al-be3 (on the sale)?
أديه الكوميشن عالبيع؟

What are the terms of the purchase?
Shou henneh chrout el chreyeh?
شو هني شروط الشراية؟

I can negotiate a better interest rate.
Fyi fawid (negotiate) 3ala feydeh a7san.
فيي فاوض على فائدة أحسن.

Business

Mortgage - Kared قرض
Interest rate - Feydeh فايدة
A loan – Kared قرض
Commission - Commission كوميشن
Percent – Nesbeh نسبة
Value – 2imeh قيمه
A sale – Be3 بيع
Profit – Rebe7 ربح
Landlord – Melik El 3i2ar مالك العقار
Tenant – Mesta2jir مستأجر
The demand – El Talab الطلب
The supply – El 3ared العرض
A contract – El 3a2ed العقد
Terms - Chrout شروط
Signature – Tew2i3 توقيع
Initials – El 2a7rof el 2oula Men el 2esem الاحرف الأولى من الاسم
Stock – 2ashom أسهم
Stock broker – Semsar 2ashom سمسار أسهم
Advertisement – Di3ayeh دعاية
Ads – 2e3lenet إعلانات

The client wants to lease instead of purchasing the property.
El zboun baddo yesta2jir badel ma yechtri el 3i2ar.
الزبون بدو يستأجر بدل ما يشتري العقار.

I need a signature and an initial on the contract.
Badi 2omda wel 2a7rof el 2oula men el 2esem 3al 3a2ed.
بدي إمضا والأحرف الأولى من الاسم عالعقد.

My position in the company is marketing and I am responsible for advertising and ads.
Markazi bel cherkeh houeh bel marketing w ana mas2oul 3an el di3ayet wel 2e3lenet.
مركزي بالشركة هو بالماركيتنج وأنا مسؤول عن الدعايات والإعلانات.

I can earn a huge profit from the stock market.
Fyi 2erba7 ktir bi sou2 el 2ashom.
فيي أربح كتير بسوق الأسهم.

I need a small loan in order to pay my mortgage this month.
Badi kared zghir la 2edfa3 el kared taba3 hayda el chaher.
بدي قرض زغير لإدفع القرض تبع هيدا الشهر.

Money - Masari مصاري
Currency – 3emleh عملة
Cash – Na2di نقدي
Coins – Lirat ليرات
Change (change for a bill) – Srafeh صرافة
Credit – 2e2timen إئتمان
Tax – Daribeh ضريبة
Price – Se3er سعر
Invoice – Fetoura فاتورة
Inventory – Stock ستوك

Don't forget to bring cash with you.
Ma tensa tjib na2di ma3ak.
.ما تنسى تجيب نقدي معك

Do you have change for a $100 bill?
3andak srafit war2it 100$?
عندك صرافة ورقة 100$؟

I don't have a credit card.
Ma 3andi bita2it 2e2timen.
.ما عندي بطاقة إئتمان

The salesperson told me that there is no refund.
El biyye3 2alli (told me) 2enno (that) ma fi badal.
.البياع قالي إنه ما في بدل

This product is covered by insurance.
Hayda el mountaj mghatta (covered) bel assurance.
.هيدا المنتج مغطى بالأشورنس

This invoice contains a mistake.
Hayde el fetoura fiya ghalta (mistake).
.هيدي الفاتورة فيا غلطة

Let me check my inventory.
Khallini (let me/allow me) chayyik el stock taba3i.
.خليني شيك الستوك تبعي

Merchandise – Bda3a بضاعة
Income - Madkhoul مدخول
A refund – Badal بدل
A product – Mountaj منتج
Produced – Msanna3 مصنع
Retail – Mfarra2 مفرّق
Wholesale – Jemleh جملة
Imports – 2istirad استيراد
Exports – Tosdir تصدير
To ship – Tech7an تشحن
Shipment – Che7neh شحنة

You don't have enough money to purchase the merchandise.
Ma 3andak masari kfeyeh (enough) la techtri haydeh el bda3a.
.ما عندك مصاري كفاية لتشتري هيدي البضاعة

How much does the shipping cost and is it in US currency?
2addeh kelfit (cost) el cha7en w hal hiyeh bi 3emlit el dollar?
أدي كلفة الشحن، وهل هي بعملة الدولار؟

This product is produced in Italy.
Hayda el montaj msanna3 bi 2italia.
.هيدا المنتج مصنّع بايطاليا

I work in the export/import business.
2ana bechteghil bi tijarit el 2istirad wel tosdir.
.أنا بشتغل بتجارة الإستيراد والتصدير

What is the wholesale and retail value of this shipment?
Shou 2imet hayde el che7neh bel jemleh w bel mfarra2?
شو قيمة هيدي الشحنة بالجملة وبالمفرّق؟

There is a tax exemption on this income.
Fi 2e3fa (exemption) daribi 3a hayda el madkhoul.
.في إعفا ضريبي عهيدا المدخول

Sports - Ryada رياضة

Basketball - Basketball باسكيت بول
Soccer – Football فوت بول
Game – Moubarat مباراة
Stadium – Mal3ab ملعب
Ball – Tabeh طابة
Player – La33ib لاعب
Player – (f) La33ibeh لاعبة
To jump - Tnott تنط
To throw - Tkebb تكب
To kick - Tshout تشوط
To catch – Tol2at تلقط
Coach – Mdarrib مدرب
Coach - (f) Mdarrbeh مدربة
Referee – 7akam حكم
Competition – Mouseba2a مسابقة

I like to watch basketball games.
B7ebb 2o7dar moubarayet el basketball.
بحب أحضر مباريات الباسكيت بول.

Soccer is my favorite sport.
El football hiyeh ryadti el moufaddaleh.
الفوت بول هيي رياضتي المفضلة.

I have tickets to a football game at the stadium.
Fi 3andi ticketet la moubarat football bel mal3ab.
في عندي تكت لمباراة فتبول بالملعب.

To play basketball, you need to be good at shooting and jumping.
Ta tel3ab basketball, lezim tkoun 2awi bel tochwit wel natt.
تا تلعب باسكيت بول لازم تكون قوي بالتشويط والنط.

The coach needs to bring his team today to meet the new referee.
El mdarrib baddo yjib fari2o lyom la yet3arrafou 3al 7akam el jdid.
المدرب بده يجيب فريقو اليوم ليتعرفوا عالحكم الجديد.

Not every person likes sports.
Mech kel chakhes (person) bi 7ebb el ryada.
مش كل شخص بحب الرياضة.

Sports

Team – Fari2 فريق
Teammate – Zamil زميل
National team – Fari2 Watani فريق وطني
Opponent – Khasim خصم
Half time – 2istira7a Ben El Chawten استراحة بين الشوطين
Finals – Nihe2iyyet نهائيات
Score - Score سكور / **Scores** – Scorat سكورات
Goal - Marma مرمى
The goal – El Marma المرمى
To lose - Tekhsar تخسر
A Defeat - Khsarah خسارة
To win – Terba7 تربح
A victory – Rebe7 ربح
The looser – El Khosran الخسران
The winner – El Reb7an الربحان
Fans – Mouchajji3in المشجعين
Field – Mal3ab ملعب
Helmet - Taseh طاسة
Whistle – Soufayra صفيرة
Penalty – Darbit Jaze2 ضربة جزاء
Basket – Salleh سلة

The national team has a lot of fans.
El fari2 (team) el watani (national) 3ando ktir mouchajji3in.
الفريق الوطني عنده كتير مشجعين.

My teammate can't find his baseball helmet.
Zamili ma 3am bi le2i tasit el baseball taba3o (of his).
زميلي ما عم بيلاقي طاسة البيسبول تاعتو.

The coach and the team were on the field during half-time.
El mdarrib wel farij kenou 3al mal3ab bel 2istira7a ben el chawten.
المدرب والفريق كانوا عالملعب بالإستراحة بين الشوطين.

Our opponents went home after their defeat.
Khasimna ra7ou 3al bet men ba3d ma khosrou.
خصمنا راحوا عالبيت من بعد ما خسروا.

The player received a penalty for kicking the ball in the wrong goal.
El la33ib akhad darbit jaze2 la2enno chat el tabeh bel marma el ghalat.
اللاعب أخد ضربة جزاء لأنه شاط الطابة بالمرمى الغلط.

Athlete – Riyadi رياضي
Olympics – 2olympiade أولمبيادي
World cup – Kes El 3alam كأس العالم
Swimming – Sbe7a سباحة
Wrestling – Mousara3a مصارعة
Boxing - Moulekameh ملاكمة
Martial arts – Founoun 2iteliyeh فنون قتالية
Championship - Boutouleh بطولة
Award - Jeyzeh جايزة
Tournament – Mouseba2a مسابقة
Horse racing – Saba2 2o7sneh سباق أحصنة
Racing – Saba2 سباق

Today are the finals for the Olympic Games.
El yom el nihe2iyet taba3 el 2al3ab el 2olympiade.
اليوم النهائيات تبع ألعاب الأولمبياد.

Let's see who wins the World Cup.
Khallina nchouf min byerba7 kes el 3alam.
خلينا نشوف مين بيربح كأس العالم.

I want to compete in the cycling championship.
Baddi anafis bi boutelet el derrajet.
بدي أنافس ببطولة الدراجات.

I am an athlete so I must stay in shape.
2ana riyadi fa lezim ydall (to stay) 3andi laye2a.
أنا رياضي فلازم يضل عندي لياقة.

After my boxing lesson, I want to go and swim in the pool.
Men ba3d dars (lesson) el boxing taba3i, badi rou7 2esba7 bel piscine.
من بعد درس البوكسينج تبعي بدي روح أسبح بالبسين.

He will receive an award because he is the winner of the martial-arts tournament.
Ra7 yekhod jeyzeh la2eno houeh rebi7 mouseba2it el founoun el 2iteliyeh.
رح ياخد جايزة لأنه ربح مسابقة الفنون القتالية.

The wrestling captain must teach his team the rules of the sport.
Capitain fari2 el mousara3a lezim y3allim fari2o 2wenin el ryada.
كابتن فريق المصارعة لازم يعلم فريقو قوانين الرياضة.

I want to run on the track today.
Lezim 2erkod 3al masasr lyom.
لازم أركض عالمسار اليوم.

Bicycle - Biciclette بسكليت
Cyclist - Derraj دراج
Exercise - Temrin تمرين
Fitness – Laye2a لياقة
Gym – Nedi نادي
Captain - Captain كابتن
Judge – 7akam حكم
A match – El Match الماتش
A match – Mubarah مباراة
Rules – 2wenin قوانين
Track – Masar مسار
Trainer - Mdarrib مدرب
Trainer - (f) Mdarrbeh مدربة
Pool (billiards) - Billard بلارد
Pool (swimming pool) – Piscine بسين

There is a bicycle race at the park today.
Fi saba2 biciclettet bel hadi2a lyom.
فيه سباق بسكليتات بالحديقة اليوم.
This fitness program is expensive.
Bernemij (program) el laye2a hayda ghali.
برنامج اللياقة هيدا غالي.
It's healthy to go to the gym every day.
So77i trou7 3al nedi kel yom.
صحي تروح عالنادي كل يوم.
Weightlifting is good exercise.
Rafe3 el 2at2el temrin mni7.
رفع الأثقال تمرين منيح.
I like to win in billiards.
B7ebb 2erba7 bel billiard.
بحب أربح بالبليارد.
Skating is much easier than it seems.
El skating ahwan bi ktir memma bi bayyin.
السكيتنج أهون بكتير مما ببين.
Skateboarding is forbidden here.
El tazaluj mamnou3 hon.
التزلج ممنوع هون.

Outdoor Activities - 2anchita kherjiyyeh أنشطة خارجية

Hiking – Hiking هايكنج
Hiking trail – Mamarr Lal Hiking ممر للهايكنج
Pocket knife – Sekkinet Jayb سكينة جيب
Compass – Bousleh بوصلة
Camping - Tekhyim تخييم
A camp – Moukhayyam مخيم
RV – Siyyarit Al Tekhyim سيارة التخييم
Campground – Moukhayyam مخيم
Tent – Khaymeh خيمة
Campfire – Nar El Moukhayyam نار المخيم
Matches - Kabrit كبريت
Lighter – 2edde7a قداحة
Coal – Fa7em فحم
Flame - Lahab لهب
The smoke – Dakhneh دخنة

I enjoy hiking on the trail, with my compass and my pocketknife.
Bonbosit 2a3mol hiking 3al masar, ma3 el bousleh taba3i w sekkinet el jayb.
بنبسط أعمل هايكنج عالمسار، مع البوصلة تبعي وسكينة الجيب.

Don't forget the water bottle in your backpack.
Ma tensa 2anninit (bottle) el may (water) bi chantit dahrak.
ما تنسى قنينة الماي بشنطة ضهرك.

There aren't any tents at the campground.
Ma fi khiyam bel moukhayyam.
ما في خيم بالمخيم.

I want to sleep in an RV instead of a tent.
Badi nem bi siyarit el moukhayyam, badel el khaymeh.
بدي نام بسيارة المخيم بدل الخيمة.

We can use a lighter to start a campfire.
Fina nesta3mil 2edde7a la nwalli3 nar lal moukhayyam.
فينا نستعمل قداحة لنولع نار للمخيم.

We need coal and matches for the camping trip.
Lezemna fa7em w kabrit la re7lit (trip) el tekhyim.
لازمنا فحم وكبريت لرحلة التخييم

Outdoor Activities

Fishing – Sed Samak صيد سمك
To fish – Tetsayyad Samak تتصيد سمك
Fishing pole – 2asbit Sed Samak قصبة صيد سمك
Fishing line – Khet La Sed El Samak خط لصيد السمك
Hook - Sennara صنارة
A float – 3ouwwem عويم
A weight - Wazen وزن
Bait – To3om طعم
Fishing net – Chabkit Sed شبكة صيد
To hunt – Tetsayyad تتصيد
Rifle – Baroudeh بارودة

Put out the fire because the flames are very high and there is a lot of smoke.
Tfi (turn off) el nar la2enno el lahab ktir 3ali (high) w fi ktir dakhneh.
طفي النار لأنه اللهب كتير عالي وفي كتير دخنة.

There is fog outside and the temperature is below freezing.
Fi dabab barra wel 7arara ta7et (below) el sefer (freezing).
في ضباب برة والحرارة تحت الصفر.

Where is the fishing store? I need to buy hooks, fishing line, bait, and a net.
Wen ma7al sed el samak? Badi echtri sennaret, khet lal sed, to3om, w chabakit sed.
وين محل صيد السمك؟ بدي أشتري صنارة، خيط للصيد، طعم، وشبكة صيد.

You can't bring your fishing pole or your hunting rifle to the campground of the State Park because there is a sign there which says, "No fishing and no hunting."
Ma fik tjib 2asbit el sed aw baroudit el sed taba3ak 3al moukhayyam yali mawjoud bel park la2enno 7attin 2armit, "Mamnou3 sed el samak 2aw el tasayyad".
ما فيك تجيب قصبة الصيد أو بارودة الصيد تبعك عالمخيم يلي موجود بالبارك لأنه حاطين قارمة (ممنوع صيد السمك أو التصيد).

Sailing – 2eb7ar إبحار
A sail – Chira3 شراع
Sailboat – Chakhtour Chira3i شختور شراعي
Rowing – Tejdif تجديف
A paddle – Mejdef مجداف
Motor – Moteur متور
Canoe – Canoe كنو
Kayak – Kayak كياك
Rock climbing – Tasallo2 Skhour تسلق صخور
Horseback riding – Roukoub Kheil ركوب الخيل
Ice skating – Tazalloj 3al Jalid تزلج عالجليد
Skiing – Altazahlu2 التزحلق

With a broken motor, we need a paddle to row the boat.
Ma3 moteur maksour, lezemna mejdef ta njaddif bel chakhtoura.
.مع متور مكسور، لازمنا مجداف تا نجدف بالشختورة

It's important to know how to use a sail before sailing on a sailboat.
Mhemm ta3rif kif testa3mil el chira3 2abel ma teb7or 3ala chakhtour chira3i.
.مهم تعرف كيف تستعمل الشراع قبل ما تبحر عالشختور الشراعي

In my opinion, a kayak is much more fun than a canoe.
Bi ra2yi (opinion), el kayak bi salli (fun) aktar bi ktir men el Canoe.
.برأيي الكياك بسلّي أكتر بكتير من الكنو

There are several outdoor activities here including rock climbing and horseback riding.
Fi ktir nachatet hon btedamman tasallo2 skhour w roukoub el kheil.
.في كتير نشاطات هون بتضمن تسلق صخور و ركوب الخيل

Ice skating is fun.
El tazalloj 3al jalid ktir bi salli.
.التزلج عالجليد كتير بسلّي

We are going skiing on our next vacation.
Ray7in na3mol ski bi forsetna el jeyeh.
.رايحين نعمل سكي بفرصتنا الجاي

Outdoor Activities

Diver - Chauffeur شوفير
Diver - (f) Chauffeur شوفير
Scuba diving – Ghaws غوص
Skydiving – 2afez Bil Mizalleh قفز بالمظلّة
Parachute – Parachute براشوت
Paragliding – Parapente براشوت
Hot air balloon – Mentad منطاد
Kite – Tiyyara Wara2iyyeh طيارة ورقية
Surfing - Rukub al2amwaj ركوب الأمواج
Surf board – Lo7 Lal rukub al2amwaj لوح لركوب الأمواج
Ice skating – Tazalloj 3al Jalid تزلج عالجليد
Skiing – Altazahlu2 التزحلق

Do I need to bring my scuba certification to be able to scuba dive at the reef?
Lezim jib chhedit (certification) ghaws la-2e2dir (to be able to) ghous had el che3ab (reef)?
لازم جيب شهادة غوص لا أقدر غوص حد الشعّاب؟

I have my mask, snorkel, and fins.
El mask, el snorkel wel za3enif-ma3i (fins).
الماسك و السنوركل والزعانف معي.

I don't know which is scarier, sky diving or paragliding.
Ma-ba3rif (I don't know) 2ayyeh (which) bi khawwif 2aktar, el 2afez bil mizalleh 2aw el parapente.
ما بعرف إياه بخوف أكتر، القفز بالمظلّة أو البراشوت.

My dream was always to fly in a hot-air balloon.
Deyman ken 7elmi (my dream) 2otla3 bi mentad.
دايماً كان حلمي أطلع بمنطاد.

Where is the surfboard? I want to surf the waves at the beach tomorrow.
Wen lo7 (board) rukub al-mawj ? Badi arkab el mawj (waves) bel ba7er boukra.
وين لوح ركوب الموج؟ بدي أركب الموج بالبحر بكرا.

Electrical Devices - 2ajhizeh Kahroube2iyyeh أجهزه كهربائية

Electricity - Kahraba كهربا
Electric – Kahrabji كهربائي
Appliance – Jihez جهاز
Oven – Foron فرن
Stove – Ghaz غاز
Microwave – Microwave ميكرويف
Refrigerator - Berrad براد
Freezer – Tellejeh تلاجة

He needs to pay his electric bill if he wants electricity.
Lezim yedfa3 fetourit el kahraba 2eza baddo kahraba.
.لازم يدفع فاتورة الكهربا إذا بده كهربا

I need to purchase a few things at the electronic store and at the appliance store tomorrow.
Lezim 2echtri kam (a few) chaghleh (things) men ma7al el 2elektroniyet w men ma7al el 2ajhizeh el kahroube2iyyeh boukra.
.لازم إشتري كم شغلة من محل الإكترونيات ومن محل الأجهزة الكهروبائية بكرة

I can't put plastic utensils in the dishwasher.
Ma fiyi 7ott 2adawet plastikiyyeh bel jelleyeh.
.ما فيي حط أدوات بلاستيكية بالجلاية

I am going to get rid of my microwave and oven because they are not functioning.
Baddi 2etkhallas men el microwave wel foron taba3i la2enno ma 3am yechteghlou.
.بدي أتخلص من الميكرويف والفرن تبعي لأنه ما عم يشتغلوا

The refrigerator and freezer aren't cold enough.
El berrad wel tellejeh mannon-berdin (aren't cold) kfeyeh.
.البراد والتلاجة مانن باردين كفاية

Electrical Devices

Coffee maker – Makanit 2ahweh ماكينة قهوه
Coffee pot – Bri2 2ahweh بريق قهوه
Toaster – Ma7masa محمصة
Dishwasher – Jelleyeh جلاية
Laundry machine - Ghesseleh غسالة
Laundry - Ghasil غسيل
Dryer – Nechefeh نشافة
Fan – Marwa7a مروحة
Air condition – AC أي سي
Alarm – Munabbeh منبّه
Smoke detector – Kechif El Dekhan كاشف الدخان
Remote Control – Remonte ريمونت
Battery – Bottariyyeh بطارية

The coffee maker and toaster aren't in the kitchen.
Makanit el 2ahweh wel ma7masa mannon bel matbakh.
ماكنة القهوة والمحمصة مانن بالمطبخ.

My washing machine and dryer do not function therefore I must wash my laundry at the public laundromat.
El ghesseleh wel nechefeh taba3i ma byechteghlou, menhek lezim ghassil el ghasil bi maghsal el 3am.
الغسالة والنشافة تبعي ما بشتغلوا ، من هيك لازم غسّل الغسيل بالمغسل العام.

Is this fan new?
Haydeh el marwa7a jdideh?
هيدي مروحة جديده؟

Unfortunately, the new air conditioner unit hasn't been delivered yet.
La sou2 el 7azz (unfortunately), ma-sallamou (they haven't delivered) el AC el jdid ba3d.
لا سوء الحظ ما سلّموا ال أي سي الجديد بعد.

Is that annoying sound the alarm clock or the fire alarm?
Hayda el sot el mez3ij (annoying) houeih sot munabbeh el se3a aw munabbeh el 7ari2?
هيدا الصوت المزعج هو صوت منبّه الساعة أو منبّه الحريق؟

The smoke detector needs new batteries.
Kechif (detector) el dekhan baddo bottariyet jded.
كاشف الدخان بده بطاريات جداد.

Lamp – 2andil قنديل
Stereo – Stereo ستيريو
A clock – Se3a ساعة
A watch – Se3a ساعة
Vacuum cleaner – Mekensit Kahraba مكنسة كهربا
Phone – Telephon تليفون
Text message – Riseleh رسالة
Voice message – Riseleh Sawtiyyeh رسالة صوتية
Camera – Camera كاميرا

The clock is hanging on the wall.
El se3a m3alla2a (hanging) 3al 7et (wall).
الساعة معلقة عالحيط.

The cordless stereo is on the table.
El stereo yalli bala (without) chrit 3al tawleh.
الستيرو يلي بلا شريط عالطاولة.

I still have a home telephone.
Ba3d 3andi telephon el bet.
بعد عندي تليفون البيت.

I need to buy a lamp and a vacuum cleaner today.
Badi 2echtri 2andil w mekensit kahraba lyom.
بدي أشتري قنديل ومكنسة كهربا اليوم.

In the past, cameras were more common. Today, everyone can use their phones to take pictures.
Men-zamen (in the past), el camerat kenou metwejdin (common/present) aktar. Lyom, kel el 3alam fiyon yesta3emlou telephoneton ta ysawwrou.
من زمان الكاميرات كانوا موجودين أكتر، اليوم فيون يستعملوا تليفوناتن تا يتصوروا.

You can leave me a voice message or send me a text message.
Fik tetrekli (to leave me) riseleh sawtiyyeh aw teb3atli riseleh.
فيك تتركلي رساله صوتية أو تبعتلي رسالة.

Electrical Devices

Flashlight - Pil بل
Light – Daw ضو
Furnace - Foron فرن
Heater – Sekhan سخان
Cord – Chrit شريط
Charger – Chei7en شاحن
Outlet – Makhraj مخرج
Headsets – Semme3at سماعات
Doorbell – Jaras El Beb جرس باب
Lawn mower – Jezzezet 7achich جزازة حشيش

The lights don't function when there is a blackout therefore I must rely on my flashlight.
El 2odowyeh ma byechteghlou wa2et tkoun ma2tou3a el kahraba, menhek lezim e3temid (to rely) 3al pil taba3i.
الضواية ما بشتغلوا وقت تكون مقطوعة الكهربا ، من هيك لازم أعتمد عالبل تبعي.

I can't hear the doorbell.
Ma 3am besma3 jaras el beb.
ما عم أسمع جرس الباب.

There is a higher risk of causing a house fire from an electric heater than a furnace.
Fi khatar 2aktar 2enno tsabbib 7ari2 bel bet men wara deffeyit el kahraba aktar men el foron.
في خطر إنه تسبب حريق بالبيت من ورا دفاية الكهربا أكتر من الفرن.

I need to connect the cord to the outlet.
Lezim 2ousol el chrit bel makhraj.
لازم أوصل الشريط بالمخرج.

His lawnmower is very noisy.
Jezzezit el 7achich ktir 3am ta3mol dajjeh.
جزازة الحشيش كتير عم تعمل ضجة.

Why is my headset on the floor?
Leh el semme3at taba3i 3al 2ared (ground).
ليه السماعات تبعي عالأرض.

Tools – 3eddeh عدة

Toolbox – 3elbit 3eddeh علبة عدة
Carpenter – Nejjar نجار
Hammer – Matra2a مطرقة
Saw - Menchar منشار
Axe – Balta بلطة
A drill – Ma2da7 مقداح
To drill – Te2da7 تقدح
Nail - Mesmar مسمار
A screw – Berghi برغي
Screwdriver – Mfakk Braghi مفك براغي
A wrench – Mefte7 2englizi مفتاح انجليزي
Pliers - Kamasheh كماشة

The carpenter needs nails, a hammer, a saw, and a drill.
El nejjar baddo msemir, matra2a, menchar w ma2da7.
النجار بده مسامير، مطرقة و منشار ومقدح.

The string is very long. Where are the scissors?
El kheit (string/line) ktir tawil. Wen el m2ass?
الخيط كتير طويل، وين المقص؟

The screwdriver is in the toolbox.
Mfakk el braghi bi 3elbit el 3eddeh.
مفك البراغي بعلبة العدة.

This tool can cut through metal.
Haydeh el adet bet2oss el 7adid.
هيدي الأداة بتقص الحديد.

The ladder is next to the tools.
El sellom 7add (next to) el 3eddeh.
السلم حد العدة.

How can I fix this machine?
Kif fyi salli7 (to fix) hayde el makana?
كيف فيي صلّح هايدي الماكنة؟

Paint brush – Fercheyit Dhen فرشاية دهان
To paint - Tedhan تدهن
The paint – El dhen الدهان
Ladder – Sellom سلّم
Rope – 7abel حبل
String – Kheit خيط
A scale – Mizen ميزان
Measuring tape - Meter متر
Machine – Makana ماكنة
A lock – 2efel قفل
Locked – Ma2foul مقفول
To lock – Te2fol تقفل
Equipment – Ma3addet معدات
Broom - Mekenseh مكنسة
Dust pan – Majroud مجرود
Bucket – Satel سطل
Sponge - Lifeh ليفة
Mop – Mamsa7a ممسحة
Shovel - Rafech رفش
A trowel – Majrafeh مجرفة

I must buy a brush to paint the walls.
Lezim 2echtri fercheyeh la 2edhan el 7itan.
لازم أشتري فرشاية لإدهن الحيطان.

The paint bucket is empty.
Satel el dhein fadi.
سطل الدهان فاضي.

It's better to tie the shovel with a rope in my pick up truck.
Mn el afdal enno torbot (to tie) el rafech bi 7abel bel pick up taba3i.
من الأفضل إنه تربط الرفش بحبل بالبيك أب تبعي.

The broom and dust pan are with the rest of my cleaning equipment.
El mekenseh wel majroud ma7toutin ma3 be2i 2adawet el tondif.
المكنسة والمجراد مع باقي أدوات التنضيف.

Where did you put the mop and the bucket?
Wen 7attet el mamsa7a wel satel?
وين حطيت الممسحة والسطل.

Car - Siyyara سيارة

Engine – Moteur متور
Ignition – Marche مرش
Steering wheel – Direction ديركشن
Automatic – Automatic أتوماتك
Manual – Yadawi يدوي
Gear shift – Ghyar Vitesse غيار فتسي
Seat – Ma23ad مقعد
Seat belt – 7izem 2amein حزام الأمان
Airbag – Airbag إيرباج
Brakes – Frem فريم
Hand brake – Frem 2id فريم إيد

When driving, both hands must be on the steering wheel.
Lama (when) tkoun 3am betsou2 (driving), el 2idten lezim ykounou 3al direction.
لما تكون عم بتسوق ، الإيدين لازم يكونوا عالدايركشن.

I must take my car to my mechanic because there is a problem with the ignition.
Lezim ekhod siyarti 3end el mecanicien la2enno fi mechekleh bel march.
لازم آخد سيارتي عند الميكنيكين لأنه في مشكلة بالمرش.

What happened to the engine?
Shou sarlo (happened) el moteur?
شو صرله الماتور؟

The seat is missing a seat belt.
El ma23ad ma-fiyo (there isn't / missing) 7izem 2amein.
المقعد ما فيو حزام أمان.

I prefer a gear shift instead of an automatic car.
Bfaddil sou2 vitesse badeil siyara automatic.
بفضل سوق فيتسي بدل سيارة أوتوماتك.

The brakes are new in this vehicle
El frem jdid bi haydeh el siyara.
الفريم جديد بهيدي السيارة.

This vehicle doesn't have a handbrake.
Haydeh el siyara ma 3anda frem 2id.
هيدي السيارة ما عندا فريم إيد.

There is an airbag on both the driver side and the passenger side.
Fi airbag 3al maylten, maylit el chauffeur w yalli 7ad el chauffeur.
في إيرباج ميلة الشوفير ويلي حد الشوفير.

Car

Baby seat – Car Seat كار سيت
Driver seat – Ma23ad El Chauffeur مقعد الشوفير
Passenger seat – Ma23ad El Rukkab مقعد الرگاب
Front seat – Ma23ad 2edmeni مقعد امامي
Back seat – Ma23ad Werrani مقعد وراني
Car passenger – Rekib راكب
Warning light – Flasher فلشر
Window – Chebek شباك
Button - Zerr زر
Horn (of the car) – Zammour زامور
Airbag – Airbag إيرباج
Brakes – Frem فريم
Hand brake – Frem 2id فريم إيد
Windshield – El 2zez El 2edmeni الأزاز الأودماني
Windshield wiper – Messe7it el 2zez مساحة الأزاز
Windshield fluid – Dawa Tondif El 2zez دوا تنضيف الأزاز
Rear view mirror – Mreyit El 2ariere مراية الرير
Side mirror – Mreyit El Janeb مراية الجنب
Alarm – Alarm الارم

The baby seat is in the back seat.
El car seat bel ma23ad el werrani.
الكار سيت بالمقعد الوراني.

The warning light button is located next to the stirring wheel.
Zerr el flasher mawjoud (located) 7ad el direction.
زر الفلشر موجود حد الدايركشن.

The windshield and all four of my car windows are cracked.
El 2zez el 2edmeni wel 2arba3 chbebik taba3 siyarti kello maksourin.
الأزاز الاودماني والأربع شبابيك تبع سيارتي كلن مكسورين.

I want to clean my rear-view mirror and my side mirrors.
Baddi naddif (to clean) mreyit el 2ariere w mreyit el janeb.
بدي نضّف مراية الرير ومراية الجنب.

My car doesn't have an alarm.
Siyarti ma fiya 2alarm.
سيارتي ما فيا ألارم.

The windshield wipers are new.
Messe7at el 2zez jdeid.
مسحات الإزاز جداد.

Door handle – Maskit El Beb مسكة الباب
Spare tire – Douleb El Spare دواليب السبير
Trunk – Sandou2 صندوق
Hood (of the vehicle) – Ghata El Moteur غطى الماتور
Drive license – Rokhsit Swe2a رخصة سواقة
License plate – Nomrit El Siyara نمرة سواقة
Gasoline – Benzin بنزين
Low fuel – Benzin mish kafi بنزين مش كافي
Flat tire – Douleb Mafkhout دولاب مفخوت
Crowbar – 3atleh عتلة
A (car) jack – 3afrit عفريت
Wrench – Mefte7 2englizi مفتاح انقليزي

The door handle on the driver's side is broken.
Maskit (handle) el beib elli 3ala maylet el saye2 maksoura (broken).
مسكة الباب اللي على ميلة السايق مكسورة.

Your license plate has expired.
Nomrit el siyara taba3ak kholis wa2ta.
نمرة السيارة تبعك خلص وقتا.

I want to renew my driving license today.
Baddi jaddid rokhsit el swe2a lyom.
بدي جدد رخصة السواقة اليوم.

Are the car doors locked?
Bweb el siyyara ma2foulin?
بواب السيارة مقفولين؟

Does this car have a spare tire in the trunk?
Hayde el siyyara fiya douleb spare bel sandou2?
هيدي السيارة فيا دولاب سبير بالصندوق؟

Please, close the car door.
3mol ma3rouf, sakkir beb el siyyara.
اعمل معروف سكر باب السيارة.

Where is the nearest gas station?
Wen 2a2rab m7attit benzin?
وين أقرب محطة بنزين؟

Nature - Tabi3a طبيعة

A plant – Nabteh نبتة
Forest – Ghebeh غابة
Tree - Chajra شجرة
Wood – Khachab خشب
Trunk – Jeze3 جزع
Branch - Ghoson غصون
Leaf – War2it chajar ورقة شجر
Root – Jezer جذر
Flower – Wardeh وردة
Petal – Batleh بتلة

I want to collect a few leaves during the fall.
Baddi jammi3 (to collect) shoueiyit (a few) wra2 shajar bel kharif.
.بدي جمع شوية ورق شجر بالخريف
There aren't any plants in the desert during this season.
Ma fi ay nabet bel sa7ra bi hayda el mawsam.
.ما في أي نبات بالصحرا هيدا الموسم
The trees need rain.
El chajar baddon cheteh.
.الشجر بدون شتي
The trunk, the branches, and the roots are all parts of the tree.
El jeze3 wel aghsan wel jouzour kellon 2jzaa2 men el chajra.
.الجزع و الأغصان والجذور كلن أجزاء من الشجره
My rose bushes are beautiful.
Jammeit el wared ktir 7elwin.
.جميت الورد كتير حلوين
I must trim the grass in my garden.
Lezim jezz (to trim) el 3esheb bel jnayneh 3andi.
.لازم جز العشب بالجنينة عندي
The rain forest is a nature preserve.
El ghebeh el 2istiwe2iyeh hiyeh ma7miyyeh tabi3iyyeh.
.الغابة الإستوائية هيي محمية طبيعية
Palm trees can only grow in a tropical climate.
Chajar el nakhil bass byetla3 bel jaw el 2istiwe2i.
.شجر النخيل بس بطلع بالجو الإستوائي

Blossom – Zahra زهرة
Stem – Jeze3 جزع
Seed – Bezer بزر
Rose – Wared ورد
Nectar – Ra7i2 رحيق
Pollen – Louka7 لقاح
Vegetation – Nabet نبات
Bush - Jamme جمي
Grass – 3echeb عشب
Rain forest – Ghebeh 2istiwe2iyyeh غابة استوائية
Tropical – 2istiwe2i استوائي
Palm tree – Chajrit Nakhil شجرة نخيل
Season - Mawsam موسم
Spring – Rabi3 ربيع
Summer - Seif صيف
Winter - Cheteh شيتي
Autumn – Kharif خريف

Where can I plant the seeds?
Wen fyi ezra3 (to plant) el bezer?
وين فيي أزرع البزر؟

I am allergic to pollen.
3andi 7asesiyyeh 3al louka7.
عندي حساسية عاللقاح.

The orchid needs to bloom because I want to see its beautiful petals.
El 2orkideh lezim yzahhrou la2enno badi shouf batleta el 7elwin.
الاوركيد لازم يزهّروا لأنه بدي شوف بتلاتا الحلوين.

Is the nectar from the flower sweet?
El ra7i2 taba3 el wared 7elou?
الرحيق تبع الورد حلو؟

Be careful because the plant stem can break very easily.
Ntebih (be careful) la2enno jeze3 el nabteh byenkesir bi shouleh ktir.
انتبه لأنه جزع النبتة بنكسر بسهولة كتير.

Nature

Lake – Bou7ayra بحيرة
Sea – Ba7er بحر
Ocean – Mou7it محيط
Waterfall – Chellel شلال
River - Nahr نهر
Canal - Canal شنل
Swamp – Moustan2a3 مستنقع
Mountain - Jabal جبل
Hill - Talleh تلة
Cliff - Jaref جرف
Peak – 2emmeh قمة
Rainbow – 2aws 2eza7 قوس قزح
Lightning – Bare2 برق
Thunder – Ra3ed رعد

There is a rainbow above the waterfall.
Fi 2aws 2eza7 fo2 el chellel.
في قوس قزح فوق الشلال.

The ocean is bigger than the sea.
El mou7it 2akbar men el baher.
المحيط أكبر من البحر.

From the mountain, I can see the river.
Men el jabal, fyi shouf el nahr.
من الجبل فيي شوف النهر.

Today we hope to see snow.
Lyom 3am net2ammal nshouf talej.
اليوم عم نتأمل نشوف تلج.

I see the lightning from my window.
3am shouf el bare2 men el chebbek (window) 3andi.
عم شوف البرق من الشباك عندي.

I can hear the thunder from outside.
Fyi 2esma3 el ra3ed men barra.
فيي أسمع الرعد من برا.

I can see the volcano.
Fyi shouf el berken.
فيي شوف البركان.

Cloud - Ghaymeh غيمه
Rain - Cheteh شتي
Snow – Talej تلج
Ice - Jlid جليد
Hail – Barad بَرد
Fog – Dabab ضباب
Wind - Hawa هوا
Air – Hawa هوا
Dawn - Fajer فجر
Dew – Nedeh ندى
Sunset - Maghib مغيب
Sunrise – Chourou2 شروق

There aren't any clouds in the sky.
Ma fi ghyoum bel sama.
ما في غيوم بالسما.
I want to see the sunset from the hill.
Badi shouf Maghib el chames men el talleh.
بدي شوف مغيب الشمس من التلة.
The lake has a shallow part and a deep part.
El bou7ayra fya 2osom (part) feyich w 2osom ghami2.
البحيرة فيا قسم فيش وقسم غميق.
I don't like the wind.
Ma b7ebb el hawa.
ما بحب الهوا.
The air on the mountain is very clear.
El hawa 3al jabal ktir safi (clear).
الهوا عالجبل كتير صافي.
Every dawn, there is dew on the leaves of my plants.
Kel fajer, fi nedeh 3ala wra2 el nabetat.
كل فجر في ندى على ورق النباتات.
Is this ice or hail?
Hayda talej aw barad?
هيدا تلج أو بَرد؟
I want to climb to the summit of Mont Blanc.
Badi 3arbish 3ala 2emmit el Mont Blanc.
بدي عربش على قمة المونت بلانك.

Nature

Sky – Sama سما
World – 3alam عالم
Earth – 2ared أرض
Sun - Chames شمس
Moon – 2amar قمر
Crescent - Hilel هلال
Full moon – Bader بدر
Star - Nejmeh نجمه
Planet – Kawkab كوكب
Fire - Nar نار
Heat – Chob شوب
Humidity – Rtoubeh رطوبة
Agriculture – Zira3a زراعة
Island – Jazireh جزيرة
Cave – Kahef كهف

The moon and the stars are beautiful in the night sky.
El 2amar wel njoum 7elwin be sama el lel.
.القمر والنجوم حلوين بسما الليل

The earth is a planet.
El 2ared hiyeh kawkab.
.الأرض هيي كوكب

The heat today is unbearable.
El chob lyom mech-ma7moul (impossible).
.الشوب اليوم مش محمول

At the beach there is fresh air.
Fi hawa moun3ich (fresh) 3al chatt.
.في هوا منعش عالشط

I want to sail to the island to see the sunrise.
Badi eb7or lal jazireh la shouf chrou2 el chames.
.بدي أبحر للجزيرة لشوف شروق الشمس

Parts of the cave are dry and other parts are wet.
2ajze2 men el kahef nechfeh wel 2ajze2 el ba2weh mballaleh.
.أجزاء من الكهف نياشفة والأجزاء الباقية مبللة

We live in a beautiful world.
Ne7na Men3ich bi 3alam 7elou.
.نحنا بنعيش بعالم حلو

Public park – 7adi2a 3ammeh حديقة عامة
National park – 7adi2a Wataniyyeh حديقة وطنية
Rock - Sakhra صخرة
Stone – 7ajra حجرة
Ground - 2ared أرض
Soil – Trab تراب
Sea shore – Chatt El Ba7er شط البحر
Seashell – Sadaf صدف
Horizon – 2ofok أفق
Ray – Chou3ei3 شعاع
Dry - Nechif ناشف
Wet – Mballal مبلل
Deep – Ghami2 غميق
Shallow – Feyich فيش
Weeds – 2a3cheib أعشاب
A stick – 3asayeh عصاية
Dust – Ghabra غبرة

There is dust from the fire in the park.
Fi ghabra men el 7ari2 yalli bel 7adi2a.
في غبرة من الحريق يلي بالحديقة.

I want to collect seashells from the seashore.
Baddi jammi3 sadaf men chatt el ba7er.
بدي جمّع صدف من شط البحر.

There are too many stones in the soil so it's impossible to use this area for agricultural purposes.
Fi ktir 7jar bel trab fa mousta7il (impossible) nesta3mil hayde el manta2a (area) lal zira3a.
في كتير حجار بالتراب فمستحيل تستعمل هيدي المنطقة للزراعة.

Why are there so many weeds growing by the swamp?
Lech fi ktir a3cheb 3am yotla3ou bel moustan2a3?
ليش في كتير أعشاب عم يطلعوا بالمستنقع؟

Animals - 7ayawenet حيوانات

Pet – 7ayawen 2alif حيوان أليف
Mammals – Thadyiyyet ثدييات
Dog – Kalb كلب
Dog – (f) Kalbeh كلبة
Cat – Bsen بسين
Cat – (f) Bsayneh بسينة
Parrot – Bebbagha بباغى
Pigeon – 7amemeh حمامة
Pig – Khanzir خنزير
Sheep - Kharouf خروف
Cow – Ba2ra بقرة
Bull - Tor طور

I have a dog and two cats.
3andi kaleb w bsaynten
عندي كلب و بسينتين.

There is a bird on the tree.
Fi 3asfour 3al chajra.
في عصفور عالشجره.

I want to go to the zoo to see the animals.
Baddi rou7 3ala 7adi2it el 7ayawenet la shouf el 7ayawenet.
بدي روح على حديقة الحيوانات لشوف الحيوانات.

My daughter wants a pet horse.
Benti badda 7san.
بنتي بدا حصان.

A pig, a sheep, a donkey, and a cow are considered farm animals.
El khanzir wel kharouf wel 7mar, wel ba2ra byo3tabarou (considered) 7ayawenet mazeri3 (farm).
الخنزيرو الخروف و الحمار و البقرة ، بعتبروا حيوانات مزرعة.

I want a hamster as a pet.
Badi hamster ka 7ayawen 2alif.
بدي هامستر كحيوان أليف.

Donkey – 7mar حمار
Horse – 7san حصان
Camel – Jamal جمل
Rodent – 2awarid قوارض
Mouse - Fara فارة
Rat – Jardon جردون
Rabbit – 2arnab أرنب
Hamster – Hamster هامستر
Duck - Batta بطة
Goose – Wazzeh وزة
Turkey – 7abach حبش
Chicken - Djejeh دجاجه
Rooster - Dik ديك
Poultry – Dawejin دواجن
Squirrel – Senjeb سنجاب

A camel is a desert animal.
El jamal 7ayawen sa7rawi.
الجمل حيوان صحراوي.

Can I put ducks, geese, and turkeys inside my coop?
Fyi 7ott el batt wel wazz, wel 7abach bel 7azira (coop)?
فيي حط البط و الوز و الحبش بالحظيرة؟

We have rabbits and squirrels in our yard.
3enna 2aranib w sanejib bel jnayneh taba3na (our).
عنا أرنب وسنجاب بالجنينة تبعنا.

It's cruel to keep a parrot inside a cage.
2aseweh (cruel) 2enno tkhalli (to keep) el bebbagha bel 2afas (cage).
قاسوة إنه تخلي البباغا بالقفص.

There are many pigeons in the city.
Fi ktir 7amem bel madineh.
في كتير حمام بالمدينة.

Mice and rats are rodents.
El firan wel jradin 2awarid.
الفيران والجرادين قوارض.

Animals

Lion – 2asad أسد
Lioness – Labweh لبوة
Hyena – Dabe3 ضبع
Leopard – Fahed فهد
Panther – Nemer نمر
Cheetah – Fahed فهد
Elephant – Fil فيل
Rhinoceros – Wa7id El 2aren وحيد القرن
Hippopotamus – Faras El Naher فرس النهر

It's usually very difficult to see a leopard in the wild.
Ennak 3adatan ktir so3ob tshouf fahed bel barriyeh (wild).
.عادةً كتير صعب إنك تشوف فهد بالبرية

Cheetahs are common in certain regions of Africa and rare in others.
El fouhoud mawjoudin bi ketra bi manati2 (areas/regions) m3ayyaneh bi 2afri2ya bass nedrin bi gheir manati2.
.الفهود موجودين بمناطق معينة بأفريقيا بس نادرين بغير مناطق

Elephants and rhinoceroses are known as very aggressive animals.
El fiyala w wa7idin el 2aren ma3roufin ennon ktir 3ide2iyyin (aggressive).
.الفيلة ووحدين القرن معرفين إنن كتير عدائيين

I saw a hyena and a panther at the safari yesterday.
Chefet dabe3 w fahed bel safari mberi7.
.شفت ضبع وفهد بالسفاري مبيرح

The most dangerous animal in Africa is not the lion, it's the hippopotamus.
2akhtar 7ayawen bi 2afri2ya mech el 2asad, houeih faras el ba7er.
.أخطر حيوان بأفريقيا مش الأسد، هو فرس البحر

A wolf is much bigger than a fox.
El dib 2akbar bi ktir men el sa3lab.
.الديب أكبر من الثعلب

Are there bears in this forest?
Fi debab bel ghebeh?
في دباب بالغابة؟

Bat – Wotwat وطواط
Fox – Sa3lab ثعلب
Wolf – Dib ديب
Weasel – 2eben 3eres إبن عريس
Bear – Debb دب
Tiger – Nemer نمر
Deer – Ghazel غزال
Deer – (f) Ghazeleh غزالة
Monkey – 2ered قرد
Monkey – (f) 2erdeh قردة
Otter – 2endos قندس
Marsupial – Jrabi جرابي

Bats are the only mammals that can fly.
El watawit henneh el sadyiyyet el wa7ideh yalli fiya ttir.
.الوطاويط هني الثديات الوحيدة يلي فيا تطير

The largest member of the cat family is the tiger.
Akbar no3 ben el bsaynet houeih el nemer.
.أكبر نوع من البسينات هو النمر

Deer hunting is forbidden in the national park.
Sed (hunting) el ghezlen mamnou3 bel 7adi2a el wataniyyeh.
.صيد الغزلان ممنوع بالحديقة الوطنية

There are a lot of animals in the forest.
Fi ktir 7ayawenet bel ghebeh (forest).
.في كتير حيوانات بالغابة

There are many monkeys on the branches of the trees.
Fi ktir 2roud 3al 2aghsan el chajar.
.في كتير قرود عأغصان الشجر

An opossum isn't a rat but it's a marsupial just like the kangaroo.
El 2opossum manno jardon bass no3 men el jrabi metel (just like) el kangaroo.
.الأبوسوم منو جردون ، بس نوع من الجرابي متل الكنجارو

Bird – 3asfour عصفور
Crow – Ghorab غراب
Stork – Le2lo2 لقلق
Vulture - Neser نسر
Eagle – Neser نسر
Owl – Boumeh بومة
Peacock – Tawous طاووس
Reptile – Zawe7if زواحف
Turtle – Zele7feh زلحفاة
Snake – 7ayyeh حية
Lizard – Se7liyeh سحلية
Crocodile – Temse7 تمساح
Frog – Defda3a ضفدع

An eagle and an owl are birds of prey however vultures are scavengers.
El neser wel boumeh tuyour mufterseh bass el jaweri7 jer7a.
النسر والبومة طيور مفترسة ، بس النسور طيور جارحة.

Crows are very smart.
El gherben ktir 2azkiya (smart).
الغربان كتير أزكية.

I want to see the stork migration in Europe.
Badi shouf hejrit (migration) el le2lo2 3ala 2oroppa.
بدي شوف هجرة اللقلق على أوروبا.

Don't buy a fur coat!
Ma techtri kabbout farou!
إما تشتري كبوت فرو.

Butterflies and peacocks are colorful.
El farachet wel tawawis mlawwanin (colorful).
الفراشات والطواويس ملونين.

Some snakes are poisonous.
Fi 7ayeya semmeh (poisonous).
في حياية سامة.

Seal – Fo2meh فقمة
Whale – 7out حوت
Dolphin – Dalphin دولفين
Fish – Samkeh سمكة
Shark – 2erech قرش
Wing – Jne7 جناح
Feather – Rich ريش
Tail – Danab دنب
Fur – Farou فرو
Scales – 2echer قشر
Fins – Za3anef زعانف
Horns – 2roun قرون
Claws – Makhelib مخالب

Is that the sound of a cricket or a frog?
Hayda sot ziz aw dofda3a?
هيدا صوت زيز أو ضفدع؟

Lizards, crocodiles, and turtles belong to the reptile family.
El sa7eli wel tamesi7 wel zale7if men 3aylit (family) el zawe7if.
السحالي و التماسيح و الزحالف من عيلة الزواحف.

I want to see the fish in the lake.
Badi shouf el samak bel bou7ayra.
بدي شوف السمك بالبحيرة.

There were a lot of seals basking on the beach last week.
Ken fi ktir fo2met 3am yetchammasou 3al chatt jem3it (week) el-madyeh (past).
كان في كتير فقمات عم يتشمسوا عالشط جمعة الماضية.

A whale is not a fish.
El 7out manno samkeh.
الحوت منو سمكة.

Animals

Insect – 7achara حشرة
A cricket – Ziz زيز
Ant - Namleh نمله
Termite – Namel 2abyad نمل أبيض
A fly – Debbeneh دبانة
Butterfly – Faracheh فراشة
Worm – Doudeh دودة
Mosquito - Barghacheh برغشة
Flea - Barghout برغوت
Lice – 2amel قمل

An octopus has eight tentacles.
El 2akhtabout 3ando tmen makhelib.
الأخطبوط عنده تمن مخالب.

A jellyfish is a common dish in Asian culture.
El 2andil houeh taba2 cha3bi (common) bel 7adara (culture) el 2asyawyeh (Asian).
القنديل هو طبق شعبي بالحضارة الآسيوية.

The museum has a large collection of invertebrate fossils.
El mat7af fiyo majmou3a (collection/group) kbireh men a7afeer el rakhawiyyet
المتحف فيو مجموعة كبيرة من أحافير الرخويات.

I want to buy mosquito spray.
Baddi 2echtri spray lal barghach.
بدي أشتري سبري للبرخش.

I need antiseptic for my bug bites.
Baddi mtahhir la 3a2sat el 7acharat.
بدي مطهر لعقصات الحشرات.

I hope that there aren't any worms, ants, or flies in the bag of sugar.
Betmanna enno (that) ma ykoun fi doud, namel, aw barghach bi kis (bag) el sekkar.
بتمنى إنه ما يكون في دود، نمل وبرغش في كيس السكر.

Beetle – Khenefseh خنفسة
A roach – Sarsour صرصور
Bee – Na7leh نحلة
Spider – 3ankabout عنكبوت
Scorpion – 3a2rab عقرب
Snail – Bezzay2a بزيقة
Shrimps – 2raydis قريدس
Clams – Bala7 El Ba7er بلح بحر
Crab – Salta3un سلطعون
Octopus – 2akhtabout أخطبوط
Starfish – Nejmit Ba7er نجمة بحر
Jellyfish – 2andil قنديل

I have crabs and starfish in my aquarium.
3andi salta3un w nejmit ba7er bel 7od el-samak taba3i.
عندي سلطعون ونجمة بحر بحوض السمك تبعي.

Certain types of spiders and scorpions can possibly be dangerous.
Fi 2anwe3 m3ayyaneh men el 3ankabout wel 3a2erib mumken (possibly) ykounou khotrin.
في أنواع معينة من العنكبوت والعقارب ممكن يكونوا خطرين.

I need to call the exterminator because there are fleas, roaches, and termites in my house.
Mihtaj de22 (need) la moubid (exterminator) el 7acharet la2enno fi ktir bareghit w srasir, w namel 2abyad bel bet 3andi.
محتاج دق لموبيد الحشرات لأنه في كتير براغيت و صراصير ونمل أبيض بالبيت عندي.

Bees are very important for the environment.
El na7let ktir mhemmin lal bi2a (environment).
النحلات كتير مهمين للبيئة.

Is there a snail inside the shell?
Fi bezzay2a bi 2aleb el sadafeh (shell)?
في بزيقة بقلب الصدفية؟

Beetles are my favorite insects.
El khanefis henneh (they are) 7acharati el moufaddalin (favorite).
الخنافس هني حشراتي المفضلة.

Religion - El din الدين

Holidays – 2a3yed أعياد
Traditions/customs – Ta2elid تقاليد
God – 2allah الله / **God** – Rab رب
Bible – 2enjil أنجيل
Old Testament – El 3ahed El 2adim العهد القديم
New Testament – El 3ahed El Jdid العهد الجديد
Adam - Adam أدم / **Eve** – 7awwa حوا
Garden of Eden – Jnaynet 3adan جنينة عدن
Heaven – Sama سما
Angels - Maleykeh ملائكة
Priest - Khouri خوري / **Priest** – 7akham حاخام
Noah – Nou7 نوح / **Ark** – Safineh سفينة

The monotheistic faiths use the bible.
El din el taw7idi byesta3eml el 2enjil.
الدين التوحيدي بستعمل الإنجيل.

We have faith in miracles.
3enna 2imen (faith) bel 3ajeyib.
عندي إيمان بالعجايب.

I must say a prayer for the holiday.
Lezim 2atli sala bi mounesabit el 2a3yed.
لازم أتلي صلاة بمناسبة الأعياد.

The angels came from heaven.
El maleykeh byejou (came) men el sama.
الملايكة بيجوا من السما.

Aaron, the brother of Moses, was the first priest.
Haroun, khayyo la mousa, ken 2awwal khouri.
هارون، خيو لموسى، كان أول خوري.

The story of Noah's Ark and the flood is very interesting.
2ossit (story) safinit nou7 wel fayadan (flood) ktir mousira (interesting).
قصة سفينة نوح والفيضان كتير مؤثرة.

Adam and Eve were the first humans and they lived in the Garden of Eden.
Adam w 7awwa kenou 2awwal nes (humans) wa 3echou (they lived) bi jnaynit 3adan.
آدم وحوا كانوا أول ناس وعاشوا بجنينة عدن.

To pray - Tsalli تصلّي

Prayer – Sala صلاة
Blessing - Barakeh بركة
To bless - Tberik تبارك
Holy – 2eddis قديس
Holy – (f) 2eddiseh قديسة
Faith – 2imen إيمان
Moses - Mousa موسى
Prophet - Nabi نبي
Messiah – Masi7 مسيح
Miracle – 2o3joubeh أعجوبة
Ten commandments – El Wasaya El 3achra الوصايا العشرة
The five books of Moses – El Ketob El Khamseh Taba3 Mousa الكتب الخمسة تبع موسى
Genesis – Sefr El Tekwin سفر التكوين
Exodus - Khourouj خروج
Leviticus – Sefr El Lawiyyin سفر اللاويين
Deuteronomy – Tasniya تثنية

What is your religion?
Shou diyentak?
شو ديانتك؟

Moses had to climb up on Mount Sinai to receive the Ten Commandments from God.
Mousa idtar y3arbich 3ala jabal Sina' la yetla22a el wasaya el 3achra men 2allah.
موسى اضطر يعربش على جبل سينا ليتلقى الوصايا العشرة من الله.

The Five Books of the Moses are Genesis, Exodus, Leviticus, Numbers, and Deuteronomy.
Ketob Mousa el khamseh henneh, sefer el tekwin, el khourouj, el lawiyyin, el 2ar2am, wel tasniya.
كتب موسى الخمسة هني، سفر التكوين، الخروج، اللاويين، الأرقام والتثنية.

Moses was considered as the prophet of all prophets.
Mousa ken yo3tabar nabi kel el 2anbiya.
موسى كان يعتبر نبي كل الأنبيا.

The three forefathers are Abraham, Isaac, and Jacob.
El 2aslef (forefathers) el tleteh henneh 2ibrahim, 2is7a2, w ya32oub.
الأسلاف التلاتة هني إبراهيم، إسحاق، ويعقوب.

Christian Religion – El Diyeneh El Masi7iyyeh الديانة المسيحية

Religion

Church - Kniseh كنيسة
Cathedral – Katedra2iyyeh كاتدرائية
Catholic - Catholic كاثوليك
Christian – Masi7i مسيحي / **Christian** – (f) Masi7iyyeh مسيحية
Christianity – El Masi7iyyeh المسيحية
Catholicism – El Katolikiyyeh الكثوليكية
Jesus – Yasou3 يسوع
A cross – Salib صليب
Priest – Khouri خوري
Monastery – Der دير
Saint – 2eddis قديس / **Saint** – (f) 2eddiseh قديسة
Nun - Rahbeh راهبة
Holy – M2addas مقدس
Holy water – Mayy M2addaseh ماي مقدسة
To sin - Yokhti يخطّي
A sin – Khatiyyeh خطيئة

The church is open today.
El kniseh maftou7a lyom.
الكنيسه مفتوحة اليوم.

Jesus is the son of God.
El masi7 2eben 2allah.
المسيح ابن الله.

I have a gold necklace with a cross.
3endi 3a2ed (necklace) dehab ma3 salib.
عندي عقد دهب مع صليب.

The nuns live in the monastery.
El rahbet bi 3ichou bel deir.
الراهبات بعيشوا بالدير.

I went to pray in the cathedral.
Re7et (I went) la salli bel katedra2iyyeh.
رحت لصلّي بالكتيدرائية.

The priest baptized the baby in the holy water.
El khoury 3ammad el walad bel mayy el m2addaseh
الخوري عمّد الولد بالماي المقدسة.

Peter is a famous saint in Christianity.
Boutros 2eddis machhour (famous) 3end el masi7iyyeh.
بطرس قديس مشهور عند المسيحية.

Christmas – 3id El Miled عيد الميلاد

Christmas eve – Laylit 3id El Miled ليلة عيد الميلاد
Christmas tree – Chajrit 3id El Miled شجرة عيد الميلاد
New Year – Sent Jdideh سنة جديدة
Merry Christmas – Miled Majid ميلاد مجيد
Easter – Foso7 فصح
Chapel – Kniseh Zghireh كنيسة زغيرة
Islam - Islem إسلام
Muslim - Meslim مسلم / **Muslim** - (f) Meselmeh مسلمة
Mosque – Jemi3 جامع
Hindu - Hendousi هندوسي
Buddhist - Budi بوذي
Temple – Ma3bad معبد
Jew - Yahoud يهود (f) Yahoudiyyeh يهودية
Religious - Metdayyin متدين
Religious - (f) Metdayneh متدينة
Monotheism – Taw7id توحيد

Christians love to celebrate Christmas.
El masi7iyyeh bi 7ebbou y3aydou 3id el miled.
المسيحية بحبوا يعيدوا عيد الميلاد.

I need to turn on the lights on my Christmas tree for Christmas Eve.
Badi dawwi (turn on) el 2odowyeh (lights) elli 3ala chajrit el miled 3a 3id el miled.
بدي ضوي الأضوية اللي على شجرة الميلاد عيد الميلاد.

Two more weeks until Easter.
Fi jeme3ten (two weeks) ba3d la 3id el foso7.
في جمعتين بعد لعيد الفصح.

Merry Christmas and Happy New Year to all my friends and family.
Miled majid w 3am sa3id la kell as7abi w 3ayelti.
ميلاد مجيد وعام سعيد لكل صحابي وعيلتي.

Muslims pray at the mosque.
El mislmeen bi sallou bel jemi3.
المسلمين بصلّوا بالجامع.

In Islam they must pray five times a day.
3ad el 2islem lezim ysallou khams marrat bel nhar.
عند الإسلام لازم يصلوا خمس مرات بالنهار.

Wedding and Relationship - Zawej w 3ala2a زواج وعلاقة

Religion

Wedding – Zawej زواج
Wedding hall – Salit 3eres صالة عرس
Married – Mjawwaz مجوز
Civil wedding – Zawej Madani زواج مدني
Bride – El 3arous العروس
Groom – El 3aris العريس
Husband - El Joz الزوج
Wife – El Mara المرة
Ceremony – El 2e7tifel الإحتفال / **Reception** – 2este2bel استقبال
Chapel – Kniseh Zghireh كنيسة زغيرة
Engagement – Khotbeh خطبة
Engagement ring – Khetim El Khotbeh خاتم خطوبة
Wedding ring – Khetim El Zawej خاتم الزواج

When is the wedding?
2aymata el 3eres?
إيمتى العرس؟

We are having the service in the chapel and the reception in the wedding hall.
Ra7 na3mol el mounesabeh bel kniseh el zghireih wel 2este2bel bi salit el 3eres.
راح نعمل المناسبة بالكنيسة الزغيرة والاستقبال بصالة العرس.

Three civil weddings are taking place at the courthouse today.
Tlat a3ras madaniyyeh (civil) baddon yen3emlou bel ma7kameh (courthouse) lyom.
تلات أعراس مدنية بدن ينعملوا بالمحكمة اليوم.

The bride and groom received many presents.
El 3arous wel 3aris tla2ou ktir hadeya (presents).
العروس والعريس تلقوا كتير هدايا.

This is my engagement ring and this is my wedding ring.
Hayda khetimi el khotbeh w hayda khetimi el zawej.
هيدا خاتمي الخطوبة وهيدا خاتمي الزواج.

They are finally married so now it's time for the honeymoon.
Wa 2akhiran tjawwazou w halla2 (now) sar wa2et chaher el 3asal.
وأخيراً تزوجوا و هلأ صار وقت شهر العسل.

Anniversary – 3id عيد
Honeymoon – Chaher El 3asal شهر عسل

Fiancé – El Khatib الخطيب
Fiancé – (f) El Khatibeh الخطيبة
Valentine day – 3id el 7ub عيد الحب
Love – El 7obb حب
To love – T7ebb تحب
In love – Maghroum مغروم

I am in love with her.
2ana maghroum fiya.
أنا مغرم فيا.

I am in love with him.
2ana maghroumeh fi.
أنا مغرمة في.

I love her (male to female).
B7ebba.
بحبا.

I love him (female to male).
B7ebbo.
بحبه.

I love you.
B7ebbak.
بحبك.

Our anniversary is on Valentine's Day.
3idna 3a nhar 3id el 7ub.
عيدنا عنهار عيد الحب.

He decided to propose to his girlfriend. She said "yes" and now they are engaged.
2arrar yet2addam la rfi2to. 2alit "Eh" w henneh halla2 makhtoubin.
قرر يتقدم لرفيقتو، قالت آه، وهني هلأ مخطوبين.

He is my fiancé now. Next year he will be my husband.
Houeh khatibi halla2. Sent (year) el-jeyeh (next/future) bi sir (to become) jawzi.
هوي خطيبي هلأ، سنة الجاية بصير زوجي.

Boyfriend – Sa7ib صاحب
Girlfriend – Sa7bi صاحبة

To hug – Toghmor تُغمر
A hug – Ghamra غمرة
To kiss – Tbawwis تبوس
A kiss – Bawseh بوسة
Single – 2a3zab أعزب
Divorced – (m) Mtalla2 مطلق
Divorced – (f) Mtalla2a مطلقة
Widow – (m) 2armal أرمل
Widow – (f) 2armaleh أرملة
Romantic – Romansi رومنسي
Darling – 7abibi حبيبي
Darling – (f) 7abibti حبيبتي
A date – Maw3ad موعد
A (romantic) relationship – 3ale2a 3atifiyyeh علاقة عاطفية
A (non-romantic) relationship – 3ale2it so7beh علاقة صحبة

You are very romantic.
2enta ktir romansi.
.إنت كتير رومنسي

They have a very good relationship.
3andon 3ale2a ktir mni7a.
.عندن علاقة كتير منيحة

I am single because I divorced my wife.
2ana 2a3zab la2enni talla2et marti.
.أنا أعزب لأني طلقت مرتي

She is my darling and my love.
Hyeh 7obbi w gharami.
.هيي حبي وغرامي

I want to kiss you and hug you in this picture.
Badi bousak w 2oghomrak bi haydeh el soura.
.بدي بوسك و أغمرك بهيدي الصورة

The husband and wife are in a relationship.
El joz wel mara bi 3ale2a.
.الجوز والمرة بعلاقة

Politics – Siyeseh سياسة

Flag – 3alam علم
National anthem – Nachid Watani نشيد وطني
Nation – 2emmeh أمة
National – Watani وطني
International – Douwali دولي
Local – Ma7alli محلي
State – Wileyeh ولاية
Symbol – Ramez رمز
Peace – Salem سلام
Country – Balad بلد
County – Mou2ata3a مقاطعة
Campaign – 7amleh حملة
Independence – 2este2lel استقلال

This is a political movement which is supported by the majority.
Hayde 7arakeh siyesiyyeh mad3oumeh (supported) men el 2aktariyyeh.
هيدي حركة سياسية مدعومة من الأكترية.

This flag is the national symbol of the country.
Hayda el 3alam houeih el ramez el watani taba3 (of the) el balad.
هيدا العلم هو الرمز الوطني تبع البلد.

This is all politics.
Hayde kella siyeseh.
هيدي كلّا سياسة.

Most countries have a national anthem.
2aktariyyet el bledan 3andon nachid watani.
أكتيرية البلدان عندن نشيد وطني.

There is a difference between state law and local law.
Fi fare2 (difference/separation) ben 2enoun el wileyeh wel 2enoun el ma7alli.
في فرق بين قانون الولاية والقانون المحلي.

This is a political campaign to demand independence.
Hayde 7amleh siyesiyyeh la yettalab (to demand) bel 2isti2lel.
هيدي حملة سياسة ليطالب بالإستقلال.

Century – 2aren قرن
Majority – 2aktariyyeh أكترية
Annexation – Dam ضم
Strategic – Stratiji استراتيجي
Plan – Khotta خطة
Decision – 2arar قرار
Patriot – Watani وطني
Democracy – Dimoukratiyyeh ديمقراطية
Movement – 7arakeh حركة
Politician - Siyesi سياسي
Politician - (f) Siyesiyyeh سياسية
Politics – Siyeseh سياسة
To vote – Ysawwit يصويت
Majority – 2aktariyyeh أكترية
Party – 7ezeb حزب
Veto – Veto فيتو
Impeachment – 3azel عزل
Convoy – Mawkab موكب
Racism – 3onsoriyyeh عنصرية
Fascism – Fachiyyeh فاشية

Both parties want to veto the impeachment inquiry.
El 7ezben baddon y7ottou veto 3ala el ta72i2 taba3 el 3azel.
.الحزبين بدن يحطوا فيتو على التحقيق تبع العزل

I want to see the presidential convoy.
Badi chouf el mawkab (convoy) el ri2esi.
.بدي شوف الموكب الرئاسي

We support democracy and are against fascism and racism.
Ne7na mned3am (to support) el dimoukratiyyeh w dodd el fachiyyeh wel 3onsoriyyeh.
.نحنا مندعم الديمقراطية وضد الفاشية والعنصرية

He is a patriot of the nation.
Houeh 7adan watani men el 2emmeh.
.هو حدن وطني من الأمة

The annexation plan was a strategic decision.
Khottit (plan) el dam kenit 2arar (decision) stratiji.
.خطة الضم كانت قرار استراتيجي

Legal – 2enouni قانوني
Law – 2enoun قانون
Illegal – Mech 2enouni مش قانوني
Execution (to kill) – 2e3dem إعدام
Spy – Tajassos تجسس
Amnesty – 3afou عفو
Republic – Joumhouriyyeh جمهورية
Dictator – Dictateuri دكتاتوري
Treason – Khiyeneh خيانة
Resistance – Mou2ewameh مقاومة
Members – 2a3da2 أعضاء
Candidate – Mouracha7 مرشّح
Election – 2entikhebet انتخابات
Poll – Toswit تصويت

There were many protests and riots today.
Fi ktir mouzaharat w 2a3mel chaghab lyom.
.في كتير مظاهرات وأعمال شغب اليوم

The civilian population wanted a revolution.
El sekken el madaniyyin kan baddon thawra.
.السكان المدنيين كان بدن ثورة

The politicians want to ask the president to give the captured spy amnesty.
El siyesiyyin baddon yotolbou (ask) men el ra2is ya3ti 3afou lal jesous yalli nla2at (captured).
.السكان بدن يطلبوا من الرئيس يعطي عفو للجاسوس يلي انلقط

Although he was the brutal dictator of the republic, in private he was a nice person.
Ma3 2enno ken dictator el joumhouriyyeh el 2asi, bas sha5siyan ken chakhes latif (nice).
.مع إنه كان ديكتاتور الجمهورية القاسي ، بس شخصياً كان شخص لطيف

I want to go to the election polls to vote for the new candidate.
Badi rou7 3ala el toswit taba3 el 2intikhebet la sawwit lal mracha7 el jdid.
.بدي روح على التصويت تبع الإنتخابات لصوّت للمرشح الجديد

All the members of the resistance were accused of treason and had to ask for political asylum.
Kel 2a3da2 el mou2ewameh kenou mouttahamin (accused) bel khiyeneh w ttarrou yotolbou loujou2 siyesi.
.كل أعضاء المقاومة كانوا متهمين بالخيانة والتواطؤ واضطروا يطلبوا لجوء سياسي

Citizen - Mouwatin مواطن
Citizen - (f) Mouwatineh مواطنة
Resident - Moukim مقيم
Resident - (f) Moukimeh مقيمة
Immigrant - Mouhejir مهاجر
Immigrant - (f) Mouhejira مهاجرة
Public – 3am عام
Private – Khas خاص
Government – 7ukumeh حكومة
Revolution – Thawra ثورة
Civilian – Madani مدني
Population – Sekken سكان
Socialism – 2ichtirakiyyeh اشتراكية
Communism – Chouyou3iyyeh شيوعية
Protest - Mouzaharat مظاهرات
Riot – Chaghab شغب
International law – El 2enoun El Douwali القانون الدولي
Human rights – 7ou2ou2 El 2insen حقوق الإنسان
Punishment – 3i2ab عقاب
Torture – Te3zib تعزيب

In some countries torture and execution is a common form of legitimate punishment.
Bi ba3d el belden el te3zib wel 2e3dem henneh tari2a (forms/ways) 3adiyyeh lal 3i2ab el char3i.
ببعض البلدان التعزيب والإعدام هني طرق عادية للعقاب الشرعي.

This is a violation of human rights and international law.
Hayda khare2 (violation) la 7ou2ou2 el 2ensen (human) wel 2anoun el douwali.
هيدا خرق لحقوق الإنسان وللقانون الدولي.

Communism and socialism were popular in the 19th century.
El chouyou3iyyeh wel 2ichtirakiyyeh kenou ktir cha3biyyin bel 2aren el tesata3ch (19th).
الشيوعية والإشتراكية كانوا كتير شائعين بالقرن التاسع عشر.

In which county is this legal?
Bi 2ayya (which) balad hayda 2enouni?
بأي بلد هيدا قانوني؟

President – Ra2is El Joumhouriyyeh رئيس الجمهورية
Statement – Bayen بيان
Presidential – Ri2esi رئاسي
Vice president – Neyib El Ra2is نائب رئيس
Defense minister – Wazir El Dife3 وزير دفاع
Interior minister – Wazir El Dekhliyyeh وزير الداخلية
Exterior minister – Wazir El Kherjiyyeh وزير الخارجية
Prime minister – Ra2is El Wezara رئيس الوزرا
Campaign – 7amleh حملة
United Nations – El 2oumam El Moutta7ideh الأمم المتحده
United States – 2amerka أميركا
European Union – El 2itti7ad el 2oroppi الإتحاد الأوروبي
Biased – Men7ez منحاز
Condemnation – 2ideneh إدانة
Resolution – 2arar قرار

They want to appoint him as defense minister.
Baddon y3aynouh (to appoint) wazir dife3.
.بدن يعينوه وزير الدفاع

In some countries other than the United States, they have a prime minister, interior minister, and exterior minister.
Be ba3d el douwal gheir 2amerca, 3andon ra2is wouzara, wazir dekhliyyeh, w wazir kherjiyyeh.
.ببعض بالدول غير أميركا عندن رئيس وزرا، وزير داخلية، ووزير خارجية

I want to meet the president and the vice president.
Badi 2elte2i (to meet) bel ra2is w neyib (deputy) el ra2is.
.بدي التقي بالرئيس ونائب الرئيس

The United Nations is located in New York.
El 2oumam el moutta7ideh ma7alla bi New York.
.الأمم المتحدة محلّا بنيويورك

I am a United States citizen and a resident of the European Union.
2ana mouwatin 2amarkeni w moukim bel 2itti7ad el 2oroppi.
.أنا مواطن أمريكي ومقيم بالإتحاد الأوروبي

The resolution is biased.
El 2arar met7ayyiz.
.القرار متحيز

This was an official condemnation.
Hayde kenit 2ideneh rasmiyyeh (an official).
.هيدي كانت إدانة رسمية

Captured – Mal2out ملقوط
To capture – Tel2at تلقط
Political asylum – Loujou2 Siyesi لجوء سياسي
Ambassador - Safir سفير
Ambassador - (f) Safira سفيرة
Embassy – Safara سفارة
Consulate – 2onsoliyyeh قنصلية
Unilateral – Men Jenib Wa7ad من جنب واحد
Bilateral – Soune2i ثنائي
Treaty – Mou3ehadeh معاهدة
Rebels – Souwwar ثوار
Sanctions – 3ou2oubeit عقوبات
Coup – 2in2ileb انقلاب

This is the ambassador's residence and it is located near the embassy.
Hayda bet el safir w houwi 7add el safara.
هيدا بيت السفير و هو حد السفارة.

I need the phone number and address of the consulate.
Badi ra2em telephon w 3enwen el 2onsoliyyeh.
بدي رقم تليفون و عنوان القنصلية.

Are consular services available today?
Khadamet (services) el 2onsol metwafra (available) lyom?
خدمات القنصل متوفرة اليوم؟

The international peace treaty needs to include both sides.
Mou3ehadit el salem el douwaliyyeh lezim tetdamman el jenben (both sidees).
معاهدة السلام الدوليه لازم تضمن الجانبين.

According to the government, the rebels carried out an illegal coup.
Bel nesbeh (according to) lal 7koumeh, el souwwar naffazou (carried out) 2in2ileb mech 2anouni.
بالنسبة للحكومة ، الثوار نفذوا انقلاب مش قانوني.

They must impose sanctions against that country.
Lezim yofordou (to impose) 3ou2oubet dodd (against) hayda el balad.
لازم يفرضوا عقوبات ضد هيدا البلد.

Military – 3askar عسكر

Army – Jeich جيش
Armed forces – 2ouwet Mousalla7a قوات مسلحة
Air force – 2ouwwet Jawwiyeh قوات جوية
Military aircraft – Tiyyara 3askariyyeh طيارة عسكرية
Soldier – 3askari عسكري
Troops – 3asekir عساكر
A force – 2ouwweh قوة
Ground forces – 2ouwwet Barriyeh قوات برية
Base – 2e3deh قاعدة
Headquarter – El Ma2arr المقر
Intelligence – 2estekhbarat الاستخبارات
Ranks – Retab رتب
Border crossing – Ma3bar 7doudi معبر حدودي

I want to enlist in the military.
Baddi 2elte7i2 bel jeich.
.بدي ألتحق بالجيش

This base is designated for military aircrafts only.
Haydeh el 2e3deh mkhasasa lal tayaran el 3askari bass (only).
.هاي القاعدة مخصصة للطيران العسكري بس

That is the headquarters of the enemy.
Hayda ma2ar el 3adou.
.هيدا مقر العدو

This country has a powerful air force.
Hayda el balad 3ando 2ouwwet jawwiyeh 2awiyyeh.
.هيدا البلد عنده قوات جوية قوية

They need to enlist reserve forces for the war.
Lezim yelte7i2 2ouwwet 2e7tiyat kermel-el (for the) 7areb.
.لازم يلتحق قوات احتياط كرمال الحرب

Welcome to the border crossing.
Ahla w sahla fikon bel ma3bar el 7doudi.
.أهلاً وسهلاً فيكن بالمعبر الحدودي

Military intelligence relies on important sources of information.
2estekhbarat el jeich byetteklou 3a masadir (sources) ma3loumet (information) mhemmeh.
.استخبارات الجيش بيتكلوا عمصدر معلومات مهمة

Military

Sergeant – Ra2ib رقيب
Lieutenant – Moulezim ملازم
The general – Liwe2 لواء
Commander – Ka2ed قائد
Colonel – Ra2ed رائد
Military chief of Staff – Ra2is El 2arken رئيس الأركان
Enlistment – 2Elti7e2 إلتحاق
Reserves – 2e7tiyat احتياط
War – 7areb حرب
Terrorism – 2erheb إرهاب
Terrorist – 2erhebi إرهابي
Insurgency – Tamarrod تمرد
Refugee – Leji2 لاجئ
Refugee – (f) Lej2a لاجئة
Camp – Moukhayyam مخيم
Assassination – 2eghtiyel اغتيال
Assassin – 2eghtiyel اغتيال

The military chief of staff was the target of a failed assassination attempt.
Ra2is 2arken el jeich ken hadaf la mou7ewalit 2eghtiyel fechleh (failed).
رئيس أركان الجيش كان هدف لمحاولة اغتيال فاشلة.

The sniper killed the highest-ranking lieutenant.
El 2ennas 2atal el moulezim el 2a3la ritbeh.
القناص قتل الملازم الأعلى رتبة.

The terrorist group claimed responsibility for the car-bomb attack at the refugee camp.
El majmou3a el 2erhebiyyeh 2a3lanit mas2ouliyyeta 3an houjoum 2infijar el siyyara bi moukhayyam el lej2in.
المجموعة الإرهابية أعلنت مسؤوليتها عن هجوم انفجار السيارة بمخيم اللاجئين.

It's impossible to defeat terrorism because it's an ideology.
El taghallob 3al 2erheb mousta7il la2enno houeh 3a2ideh.
التغلب عالإرهاب مستحيل لأنه هو عقيدة.

The commander of the insurgency was accused of serious war crimes.
2eyid el tamarrod ken mouttaham (accused/blamed) bi jarayim 7areb khatira (serious).
قائد التمرد كان متهم بجرايم حرب خطيرة

Airstrike - Ghara غارة
Navy – Ba7riyyeh بحرية
Fighter jet – Tiyyar Mou2etleh طيارة مقاتلة
Drone – Tiyyara Men Doun Tayyar طيارة من دون طيار
Stealth technology – Teknolojiet El Takhaffi تكنولوجيا التخفي
Tank - Debbebeh دبابة
Submarine – Ghouwwasa غواصة
Weapon – Sle7 سلاح
Bullet – Rsasa رصاصة
Grenade – 2enbleh el yada'weeya قنبلة يدوية
Bomb – 2enebleh قنبلة
Sniper – 2ennas قناص
Gun – Fared فرد
Rifle – Baroudeh بارودة
Missile – Saroukh صاروخ

The M-16 is a US-made rifle.
El M sixteen baroudeh cheghel 2amerka.
الإم سكستين بارودة شغل أمريكا.

The navy was able to intercept a missile.
El ba7riyyeh 2edrit to3torid saroukh.
البحرية قدرت تعترض صاروخ.

At the terrorist safe-house, guns, bullets, and grenades were found.
Bi makhba (safe-house) el 2erhebi nla2a (were found) bawerid w rsas w 2anebil el yada'weeya.
بمخبى الإرهابيين انلقى بواريد ورصاص وقتابل يدوية.

An intense missile attack was carried out against the supply forces that resulted in many casualties.
Sar houjoum saroukhi mukathif dodd 2ouwwet el 2emded sabbab bi 3eddit (many) 2isabet.
صار هجوم صاروخي مكثف ضد قوات الإمداد سبب بعدة إصابات.

The coalition forces struck an enemy arms depot.
2ouwwet el ta7elof 2asafit (bombed) makhzan 2asli7a lal 3adou.
قوات التحالف قصفت مخزن أسلحة للعدو.

Anti tank missile – Saroukh Moudad Lal Debbebet صاروخ مضاد للدبابات
Anti aircraft missile – Saroukh Moudad Lal Tayaran صاروخ مضاد للطيران
Shoulder fire missile – Saroukh Byondorib Men El Ketef صاروخ بينضرب من الكتف
Ammunition – Zakhira ذخيرة
Artillery – Madfa3iyyeh مدفعية
Artillery shell – 2azifet Madfa3iyyeh قاذفة مدفية
Precision missile – Saroukh Da2i2 صاروخ دقيق
Ballistic missile – Saroukh Bolisti صاروخ باليستي
Atomic bomb – 2enbleh Nawawiyyeh قنبلة نووية
Nuclear weapon – Sle7 Nawawi سلاح نووي
Weapon of mass destruction – 2asli7it Damar Chemil أسلحة دمار شامل
Chemical weapon – Sle7 Kimye2i سلاح كيماوي
Flare system – Nizam 2anebil Daw2iyyeh نظام قنابل ضوية
Supply – 2emded إمداد / **Storage** – Tekhzin تخزين
Armor – Dere3 درع

The tank fired artillery shells.
El debebbeh darabit (fired) 2azeyif madfa3iyyeh.
الدبابة ضربت قذايف مدفعية.

Shoulder-fired missiles are extremely dangerous and are hard to defend against.
El swarikh yalli btondorib men el ketef khotra ktir w ktir so3ob tdefi3 (to defend) dodda.
الصواريخ يلي بتنضرب من الكتف خطرة كتير وكتير صعب تدافع ضدا.

The flare system is meant as a defense against anti-aircraft missiles.
Nizam (system) 2anebil el daw2iyyeh ma3moul la yosta3mal ka dife3 (defend) dodd el swarikh yali dodd el tayaran.
نظام القنابل الضوئية معمول ليستعمل كدفاع ضد الصواريخ يلي ضد الطيران.

The terrorist cell fired ballistic missiles at the nuclear facility site.
El khaliyyeh el 2erhebiyyeh darabit swarikh bolistiyyeh 3ala maw2a3 moucha2a (facility) nawawiyyeh.
الخلية الإرهابية ضربت صواريخ باليستية على موقع منشأة نووية.

Atomic bombs and chemical weapons are weapons of mass destruction.
El 2anebil el nawawiyyeh wel 2asli7a el kimewiyyeh henneh 2asli7it damar chemil.
القنابل النووية والأسلحة الكيماوية هني أسلحة دمار شامل.

A target – Hadaf هدف
To target – Testahdif تستهدف
An attack – Houjoum هجوم / **To attack** – Tehjom تهجم
Intense – 2awi قوي
Mine – Leghem لغم
To shoot – T2awwis تقويص
To open fire – Tefta7 Nar تفتح نار
Fired – 2awwas قوّص
Enemy – 3adou عدو
Reconnaissance – 2estetla3 استطلاع
Missing in action – Maf2oud Bel Khedmeh مفقود بالخدمة

There is an invasion of ground forces.
Fi 2ijtiye7 2ouwwet barriyyeh.
في اجتياح قوات برية.

The soldier wanted to open fire and shoot at the invading forces.
El 3askari ken-baddo (wanted) yefta7 nar w y2awwis el 2ouwwet yali 3am tejte7.
العسكري كان بده يفتح نار ويقوّص القوات يلي عم تجتاح.

The bomb attack was considered an act of aggression and an act of war.
3tabarou (considered) el houjoum bel 2anebil ka tasarrof 3ide2i w 3amal 7arbi.
اعتبروا الهجوم بالقنابل كتصرف عدائي وعمل حربي.

The reconnaissance drone managed to infiltrate deep within enemy territory.
Tiyyarit el 2estetla3 2edrit tetsallal bi gheme2 bi-2aleb (in the heart of) manta2it el 3adou.
طيارة الاستطلاع قدرت تستطلع بغميق بقلب منطقة العدو.

The airstrike targeted an ammunition storage site.
El ghara stahdafit maw2a3 makhzan zakhira.
الغارة استهدفت موقع مخزن زخيرة.

First, we need to clear the mines.
2awal-chi (first thing), lezim nchil el 2alghem.
أول شي لازم نشيل الألغام.

Several of the submarine sailors were missing in action.
Nfa2ad ktir men el ba77ara taba3 el ghouwwasa bel khedmeh.
انفقد كتير من البحارة تبع الغواصة بالخدمة.

To infiltrate - Tetsallal تستطلع
Invasion – 2ejtiye7 اجتياح
Exchange of fire – Tabedol Niran تبادل نيران
A cease fire – Wa2ef 2etla2 Nar وقف اطلاق النار
Withdrawal – 2insi7ab انسحاب
To defeat - Tetghallab تتغلب
To surrender – Testaslim تستسلم
Victim – Da7iyyeh ضحية
Injury – 2isabeh إصابة
Deaths - Mot موت
To kill – Te2tol تقتل
Prisoner of war – Sajin 7areb سجين حرب
Act of war – 3amal 7areb عمل حرب
War crimes – Jarayim 7areb جرايم حرب
Defense – Dife3 دفاع
Attempt – Mou7ewaleh محاولة
Explosion – 2enfijar انفجار
Mortar – Hawn هاون

The mortar attack and exchange of fire caused injuries and deaths on both sides.
El houjoum bel hawn w tabedol el niran sabbab 2isabet w da7aya (loss) bel maylten.
.الهجوم بالهاون وتبادل النيران سبب إصابات وضحايا بالميلتين

The ceasefire agreement included the release of prisoners of war.
2ittife2 (agreement) wa2ef (cease) 2etla2 el nar tdamman 2etla2 (release) sara7 soujana el 7areb.
.اتفاق وقف اطلاق النار تضمّن إطلاق سراح سجنا الحرب

The army made a public statement to announce the withdrawal.
El jeich 2addam bayen-3alani (public statement) ta ye3lon (to announce) 2insi7ebo.
.الجيش قدم بيان علني تا يعلن انسحابه

There was a huge explosion as a result of the terrorist attack.
Sar fi 2infijar kbir natijit (as a result) el houjoum el 2erhebi.
.صار في انفجار كبير نتيجة الهجوم الإرهابي

If you enjoyed this book but missed "Part-1" and "Part-2" then feel free to check them out on Amazon.

Conclusion

Hopefully, you have enjoyed this book and will use the knowledge you have learned in various situations in your everyday life. In contrast to other methods of learning foreign languages, the theory in this current usage is that ever-greater topics can be broached so that one's vocabulary can expand. This method relies on the discovery I made of the list of core words from each language. Once these are learned, your conversational learning skills will progress very quickly.

You are now ready to discuss sport and school and office-related topics and this will open up your world to a more satisfying extent. Humans are social creatures and language helps us interact. Indeed, at times, it can keep us alive, such as in war situations. You might find yourself in dangerous situations perhaps as a journalist, military personnel or civilian and you need to be armed with the appropriate vocabulary.

"This is a base for military aircraft only," you may have to tell some people who try to enter a field you are protecting, or know what you are being told when someone says to you, "Welcome to the border crossing." As a journalist on a foreign assignment, you may need to quickly understand what you are being told, such as "The sniper killed the highest-ranking lieutenant." If you are someone negotiating on behalf of the army, you may need to find another lieutenant very quickly. Lives, at times, literally depend on your level of understanding and comprehension.

This unique approach that I first discovered when using this method to learn on my own, will have helped you speak the Lebanese dialect of the Arabic language much quicker than any other way.

NOTE FROM THE AUTHOR

Thank you for your interest in my work. I encourage you to share your overall experience of this book by posting a review. Your review can make a difference! Please feel free to describe how you benefited from my method or provide creative feedback on how I can improve this program. I am constantly seeking ways to enhance the quality of this product, based on personal testimonials and suggestions from individuals like you.

Thanks and best of luck,

Yatir Nitzany

Also by Yatir Nitzany

Conversational Spanish Quick and Easy

Conversational French Quick and Easy

Conversational Italian Quick and Easy

Conversational Portuguese Quick and Easy

Conversational German Quick and Easy

Conversational Dutch Quick and Easy

Conversational Norwegian Quick and Easy

Conversational Danish Quick and Easy

Conversational Russian Quick and Easy

Conversational Ukrainian Quick and Easy

Conversational Bulgarian Quick and Easy

Conversational Polish Quick and Easy

Conversational Hebrew Quick and Easy

Conversational Yiddish Quick and Easy

Conversational Armenian Quick and Easy

Conversational Romanian Quick and Easy

Conversational Arabic Quick and Easy
Modern Standard Arabic

Conversational Arabic Quick and Easy
Palestinian Dialect

....

Conversational Arabic Quick and Easy
Syrian Dialect

....

Conversational Arabic Quick and Easy
Jordanian Dialect

....

Conversational Arabic Quick and Easy
Egyptian Dialect

....

Conversational Arabic Quick and Easy
Moroccan Dialect

....

Conversational Arabic Quick and Easy
Tunisian Dialect

....

Conversational Arabic Quick and Easy
Saudi (Hejazi, Najdi & Gulf) Dialect

....

Conversational Arabic Quick and Easy
Iraqi Dialect

....

Conversational Arabic Quick and Easy
Emirati Dialect

....

Conversational Arabic Quick and Easy
Qatari Dialect

....

Conversational Arabic Quick and Easy
Kuwaiti Dialect